Consoling Thoughts

of

St. Francis de Sales

—Second Book—

*Consoling Thoughts on Trials of an Interior Life,
Infirmities of Soul and Body, etc.*

CONSOLING THOUGHTS

of

ST. FRANCIS DE SALES

—SECOND BOOK—

*Consoling Thoughts on Trials of an Interior Life,
Infirmities of Soul and Body, etc.*

*Gathered from His Writings,
And Arranged in Order, by the*
REV. PÈRE HUGUET

TRANSLATED FROM THE FRENCH
27TH EDITION

*"You cannot read anything more useful than the works of
St. Francis de Sales, in which everything is pleasing
and consoling."*—Fenelon

TAN Books
An Imprint of Saint Benedict Press, LLC
Charlotte, North Carolina

Published by Fr. Pustet & Co., New York & Cincinnati, Printer to the Holy See and the S. Congregation of Rites, in 1912, under the title *The Consoling Thoughts of St. Francis de Sales.* A French edition of this work, apparently an earlier edition, was published in Paris in 1857 as *Pensees consolantes de Saint Francois de Sales.* . . . The compiler's surname is sometimes spelled Hoguet; his first name was given as Paul in the French edition. Retypeset in 2013 by TAN Books.

Cover design by Caroline Kiser.

Cover image: *Nepomuk Takes the Confession of the Queen of Bohemia, Crespi, Giuseppe Maria* (Lo Spagnuolo) (1665–1747) / Galleria Sabauda, Turin, Italy / The Bridgeman Art Library

ISBN: 978-0-89555-214-3

Printed and bound in the United States of America.

TAN Books
An Imprint of Saint Benedict Press, LLC
Charlotte, North Carolina
2013

St. Francis de Sales' Loving Heart

"Through a great part of my soul I am poor and weak, but I have a boundless and almost immutable affection for those who favor me with their friendship. Whoever challenges me in the contest of friendship must be very determined, for I spare no effort. There is no person in the world who has a heart more tender and affectionate towards his friends than I, or one who feels a separation more acutely." —St. Francis de Sales.

"It has pleased God to make my heart thus. I wish to love this dear neighbor ever so much—ever so much I wish to love him! Oh! When shall we be all melted away in meekness and charity towards our neighbor! I have given him my whole person, my means, my affections, that they may serve him in all his wants."—St. Francis de Sales.

CONTENTS

Publisher's Preface

S T. FRANCIS de Sales was a man of great passion. Reading his thought is to know his heart. Has Holy Mother Church ever reared a child so willing and able to express his longing for perfect union with God? Has a man so learned ever presented Truth and Beauty so simply?

Words cannot fully express the Publisher's appreciation for this Gentle Saint, the Bishop of Geneva and Doctor of the Church. Saint Francis was a lawyer, a theologian, and a missionary. As a young priest, he volunteered to re-evangelize the Calvinist of Chablais, France. He preached not only with conviction, but also with unparalleled gentleness and grace. He worked tirelessly, even under the cover of night, slipping his apologetic writings beneath the doors of anti-Catholics. The Lord rewarded him with one of the most remarkable and well-documented events in Catholic history when nearly the entire population of 72,000 Calvinists returned to the Faith.

This volume, *Consoling Thoughts*, is representative of why St. Francis was so well-received in Chablais, and indeed, throughout history. Perhaps more than any other saint, St. Francis preached truth with love. His teachings, his works, and his very presence were consoling to those 72,000 lost souls of Chablais and to millions of more over the centuries. Now, then, it is our hope that they will offer consolation to a new generation of Catholics.

It is for this reason that TAN Books is proud to bring this compilation of St. Francis' writings back to print. Initially published in a single volume, we now present this work in a four volume series, carefully arranged by topic to give solace in times of darkness, or, simply in times of deep meditation.

It is the Publisher's sincere hope that *Consoling Thoughts* finds a permanent home in your library and among our long list of Saint Francis de Sales classics, including *Introduction to the Devout Life*, *Treatise on the Love of God*, *Catholic Controversies*, and *Sermons of St. Francis de Sales* (in four volumes).

Saint Francis de Sales, Doctor of the Church, *Pray For Us.*

Robert M. Gallagher, Publisher
November 19, 2012

Preface to the Sixth French Edition

By Père Huguet

SIX editions of this little work, published in a short time, tell better than any words of ours the popularity which St. Francis de Sales enjoys amongst us. Many sick and wounded souls have found in these sweet and affecting pages a heavenly consolation.

Encouraged by this success, the honor of which belongs to God and His blessed servant, we have again with pen in hand run through the works of the Bishop of Geneva, to glean carefully whatever had escaped us on our former tour. Nor has our labor been in vain; we have gathered new flowers, whose beauty and perfume yield in no respect to the first.[1] To introduce them in this edition, we have been obliged to lop off a good many of the old chapters which were so well suited to the object of the book. We have acted thus with the less regret as we have published the omitted

---

1 The author has scarcely taken anything from the *Introduction to a Devout Life,* this admirable book being in the hands of everyone.

portions, complete, in two other volumes: the *Consoling Piety of St. Francis de Sales,* and the *Month of Immaculate Mary, by St. Francis de Sales.* These two works form a complete course of consolation for all the trials of life.

We may be permitted to give a short extract from a late number of the *Catholic Bibliography,* which contained an article on *Consoling Thoughts.* The idea of publishing the article was most remote from our mind, on account of the many marks of very great kindness towards us which it bears; but remembering that the merit of this work belongs entirely to St. Francis de Sales, we have felt impelled to give at least an extract, as a new and encouraging proof of the opportuneness of our little book.

"The very title of the book," it says "pleases, and should secure a large number of readers. How many souls are there today who stand in need of being encouraged and consoled? Want of confidence is the great obstacle in the work of the Christian apostleship. Discouragement is the evil of our period, because in general the Christian life, or Sanctity, appears like a sharp mountain, which only few persons can ascend; in despair of arriving at its summit the majority of men remain below on the plains. The mere word 'sanctity' frightens. The *Lives of the Saints,* which ought to encourage, often discourage, by their list of heroic virtues; we gladly conclude that such a state of perfection is suited only to a very small number, and we remain out of the ways of sanctity for fear of not being able to walk in them.

"Blessed then be the pious author who has received the happy inspiration of assembling together the *Consoling Thoughts of St. Francis de Sales,* the sweetest and most amiable of the saints, and one of the greatest masters of the spiritual life!

"It is especially by his admirable union of firmness and mildness that St. Francis de Sales shines in the first rank of ascetic writers. Who else ever painted virtue under lovelier colors, or made it easier or more practicable? Whoever knew better how to enlighten and bring back souls that had withdrawn from God, or that wearied themselves in His service by an unreasonable fear?

"Happy then and useful inspiration [it was], to gather from his works the thoughts most fitted to enlighten pious and timorous souls, to console them, and to dilate their hearts dried up by fear! Father Huguet has given us, in this little work, the quintessence of everything that our amiable saint wrote most sweet and consoling, especially in his letters, in which that heart so good and tender, which God had formed to comfort the afflicted, is entirely revealed. The book is of the greatest assistance to the simple faithful, and to directors and confessors charged with comforting discouraged and troubled souls.

"A word now as to the method adopted. The author read, he tells us, with pen in hand, the works of the holy Bishop of Geneva; and, after noting the different passages which referred to the same subject, he arranged them in such order as to form a single chapter. A page is thus sometimes collected from seven or eight places in the saint's writings. Yet such is the connection of ideas that we scarcely perceive the labor, and everything seems to flow as from one fountainhead. As to the graceful, artless style of St. Francis de Sales, the author has lightly retouched it in some places, changing a few antiquated expressions that would be little intelligible nowadays. Without altering anything in substance, he has considered it a duty to suppress certain details and comparisons, whose want of simplicity, a common fault at present, might cloy the work. Everywhere we have the good shepherd, who, after the example of his Divine Master, instructs, cheers, and consoles, by the help of parables and similitudes, in the great art of using which perhaps he never had an equal.

"To add more clearness and authority to the book, the author has, from time to time, placed at the foot of the page some notes taken from the most esteemed writings of our greatest masters of the spiritual life, particularly Bossuet and Fenelon. These notes, happily selected, give a new value to the work. Should we now recommend it to all those whose souls have need to be encouraged and consoled—in a word, all the faithful?"

Introduction

By Père Huguet

"The writings of St. Francis de Sales are the fruit
of grace and experience."—Fenelon

THE great evil of our period is discouragement. Tempers and characters have become weak and degenerate. Everyone agrees in saying that the most common obstacle, and the one most difficult to be overcome, which all those meet who labor for the conversion of sinners and the sanctification of pious souls, is want of confidence. The great evil that Jansenism wrought in the midst of us has not yet entirely disappeared: many still believe that perfection consists only in fearing the Lord and in trembling before Him, who, in His mercy, permits us to call Him *Our Father,* and to name Him *the good God.*

The generality of authors have placed in the *Lives of the Saints* an account of their heroic virtues only, without a single word of the defects and miseries which God left in them, in order to preserve them in humility and to make them more indulgent towards their brethren; yet the history of their weaknesses would, according to the judicious remark of St. Francis de Sales, have done the greatest good to a large number of souls, who imagine that sanctity can, and should, be exempt, even in this world, from all alloy and all imperfection. It is to remedy, as far as lies in our power, these inconveniences, that we have gathered together, under appropriate headings, from the writings of the sweetest and most amiable of all the saints, those passages which are best calculated to enlighten pious souls, and to expand their hearts withered with fear.

The writings of St. Francis de Sales are admirably suited to times of trial and sadness. The soul enjoys in them an atmosphere of mild salubrity that strengthens and renews it. The doctrine there is holy and profound, under a most amiable exterior; the style adds, by its simple naïveté, to the charm of a clear and ingenuous fancy; we are instructed while we imagine ourselves distracted, and admire while we smile.

We hesitate not to say that no saint has ever contributed so much as St. Francis de Sales, by his immortal writings, to make piety loved and practiced in all classes of society.

"Under his pen," says the best of his biographers, "devotion is noble, true and rational; courtesy of manners, a spirit of sociality, all the charms of a well-ordered piety, form its cortege, if we may use the expression, and yet it is not disguised in order to appear the more agreeable. Everywhere the author's sweetness appears without weakness, and his firmness without bitterness. He teaches us to respect decorum, which he calls the gracefulness of virtue, to rise above nature without destroying it, to fly little by little towards Heaven like doves when we cannot soar thither like eagles, that is to say, to sanctify ourselves by ordinary means. There the mind contemplates truth, unveiled in majestic splendor, bedecked with maxims equally elegant and profound, clad in a style noble, flowing and natural, relieved by the justness of the expressions, sometimes fine and delicate, sometimes vivid and impressive, always graceful and varied: this is simplicity, with all the merit of beauty, for every idea is rendered by the proper word, and every word embellishes the thought. There, above all, the heart tastes an inexpressible pleasure; because the sweetness of the sentiment always seasons the precept, while the delicacy of the precaution that accompanies it secures its acceptance, and the artless candor and goodness of the author, who paints himself without intending it, make him beloved; at the same time the soul, embalmed in what it reads, deliciously participates in the sweetest and purest perfume of true piety."[1]

The style of St. Francis de Sales is a picture of his heart as much as of his mind: we feel that he loves and deserves to be loved, but that he wishes above all things that we should love God.

A special characteristic of St. Francis de Sales is that the frequent use he makes of figures and the comparisons which he endlessly multiplies, never weary. This style

---

1   *Life of St. Francis de Sales,* by M. the Curé of Saint Sulpice. This beautiful work has met with a success which surprises no one except its author, whose modesty and evangelical simplicity can alone equal his learning and his zeal for the conversion of souls.

would be clumsy in another author; with our saint it is a new pleasure, which draws away the reader and attracts him every moment, as a gentle magnet, and this with so much the more ease as the reader does not perceive it. One is led along unresistingly, yielding with pleasure to the charms of this enchanting style. An effect, so rare and wonderful, is owing not only to our saint's judicious choice of figures and comparisons, but also to his amiable character, to the sprightliness of his sentiments, and to the transports of his love for God, which burst forth even in the midst of the most abstract truths. He cannot contain the fire that consumes him; he allows it to escape by every sense. Moreover, he so well unites simplicity of diction with beauty of metaphor, that, in perusing his works, we feel the ornaments to flow from his pen without an effort on his part to seek them. A tender and compassionate soul, he is full of charity towards his friends. Let us hear him speak: "Through a great part of my soul I am poor and weak, but I have a boundless and almost immutable affection for those who favor me with their friendship. Whoever challenges me in the contest of friendship must be very determined, for I spare no effort. There is no person in the world who has a heart more tender and affectionate towards his friends than I, or one who feels a separation more acutely."

We have so often heard the following affecting words repeated, that they seem to have fallen from the mouth of the sweet Saviour Himself: "It has pleased God to make my heart thus. I wish to love this dear neighbor ever so much—ever so much I wish to love him! Oh, when shall we be all melted away in meekness and charity towards our neighbor! I have given him my whole person, my means, my affections, that they may serve him in all his wants."

This benignity, this gentleness, which breathed through the whole conduct of our saint, made St. Vincent de Paul exclaim with touching simplicity: "O my God! How good must Thou be, since the Bishop of Geneva is so good!"

It is in his works that he deposited the richest treasures of this sweet sensibility and of this playful imagination, which enabled him to lend to the driest subjects and the severest precepts of the evangelic law a charm that makes them loved even by the profane.

The French Academy proposed the writings of St. Francis de Sales as a model to all, even at a time when it extolled the faults of Corneille.

To make himself all to all, St. Francis de Sales descends to the level of the simple faithful, and there he loves to rest. Sometimes he places himself with his *Philothea* in the midst of the stormy sea of the world, and there casts out the anchor of faith; again, he takes his stand on the high road to show to the multitude, who pass indifferent and distracted along, the narrow way that leads to Heaven. We might say that he smoothes its roughness, so carefully does he conceal it under flowers. These are not deceitful flowers, by which virtue is disfigured in the endeavor to render it more attractive; they are those flowers of the soul which perfume without corrupting it, secret joys, interior consolations, ineffable delights, the anticipated inheritance of God's elect upon earth. The picture which he draws of devotion can only be compared to that of charity by

St. Paul. "In his writings," says Père de Tournemine, "we have the morality of the Sacred Scriptures and the Holy Fathers reduced to true principles and practical rules."

The doctrine of St. Francis de Sales is like a beautiful river which takes its rise in pure and elevated regions, and which, descending to the lowlands, spreads wide its banks, in order to reflect a broader expanse of Heaven; it is decked with the flowers of the prairie which it gathers on its course, and carries to the sea a tribute only of limpid and perfumed waters.

According to St. Francis de Sales, we must not be too punctilious in the practice of virtues, but approach them honestly, with liberty, in a *grosso modo* way. "Walk simply in the way of the Lord," he says, "and do not torment your mind. We must hate our defects, but with a tranquil and quiet hatred—not with a spiteful and troubled hatred—and, if necessary, have patience to witness them and to turn them to account by a holy self-abasement. For want of this, my daughter, your imperfections, which you view so closely, trouble you much, and by this means are retained, there being nothing that better preserves our defects than fretfulness and anxiety to remove them." (*Sermon for the Feast of St. Magdalen*).

He applies to himself what he counsels to others: "I know what sort of a being I am; yet even though I feel myself miserable, I am not troubled at it; nay, I am sometimes joyful at it, considering that I am a truly fit object for the mercy of God, to which I continually recommend you."

This devotion, at least in appearance so easy, naturally

pleases persons of the world, who, like the Count Bussy-Rabutin, say: "I merely wish to get into Heaven, and no higher." This nobleman, writing in another place, says: "Save us with our good Francis de Sales; he conducted people to Heaven by beautiful ways." Yet these beautiful ways were no other than the narrow way of which the Gospel speaks; only our amiable saint knew how to smooth its entrance and to hide its thorns under flowers.

St. Francis particularly excelled in comforting the afflicted and the sick; a few words falling from his heart sufficed to calm and enlighten them; his words entered into their soul as an oil of great sweetness, which moderated the heat of their malady. Let us hear him console a pious person to whom sickness was an insupportable burden: "Be not annoyed to remain in bed without meditation, for to endure the scourges of Our Lord is no less a good than to meditate. No, indeed; but it is much better to be on the cross with Jesus Christ, than merely to contemplate Him in prayer." To another, who was troubled at the sight of her miseries, he said: "When we happen to fall, let us cast down our heart before God, to say to Him, in a spirit of confidence and humility, 'Mercy, Lord! For I am weak.' Let us arise in peace, unite again the thread of our affections, and continue our work."

St. Francis de Sales was so much the better qualified to tranquilize and encourage souls inclined to diffidence and depression, as he had himself been obliged to pass through the severest trials, and arrived at the possession of peace of heart only by a total abandonment to God. "Since at every season of life, early or late, in youth or in old age, I can expect my salvation from the pure goodness and mercy of God alone, it is much better to cast myself from this moment into the arms of His clemency than to wait till another time. The greater part of the journey is over; let the Lord do with me according to His will; my fate is in His hands; let Him dispose of me according to His good pleasure."

The pious M. Olier, that great master of the spiritual life, very much esteemed St. Francis de Sales. "God," he says, "wishing to raise him up as a torch in the midst of His Church to enlighten an immense number, replenished him with the most marvelous gifts of understanding, knowledge, and wisdom, proportioned to His designs. As for his knowledge, it was evidently more than human, and the effect of the Divine Spirit."

If you wish to know Francis de Sales thoroughly, to be initiated into the most secret mysteries of that vast understanding and that perfect heart, read and re-read his *Letters,* in which every subject, from the most humble to the most sublime, from a simple how-do-you-do to a description of ecstasies and eternal beatitudes, is treated of in the style that best suits it. Read, above all, the *Letters to Madame de Chantal,* and those which treat of the *direction of souls.* Considering these admirable letters, Bossuet says: "Francis de Sales is truly sublime; there is no one among moderns with such sweetness, who has a hand so steady and experienced as his, to elevate souls to perfection and to detach them from themselves." The letter written after the death of his mother is of a primitive simplicity, and a sublime model of Christian resignation; we imagine that we hear St.

Augustine weeping over St. Monica, and the tears it makes us shed have nothing of bitterness, so sweet is the death of the just when thus related.

The learned and pious Archbishop of Cambray continually recommended the perusal of our saint's writings. "You cannot read anything more useful," says Fenelon, "than the books of St. Francis de Sales; everything there is consoling and pleasing, though he does not say a word but to help us to die. His artless style displays an amiable simplicity, which is above all, the flourishes of the profane writer. You see a man who, with great penetration and a perfect clearness of mind to judge of the reality of things, and to know the human heart, desires only to speak as a good-natured friend, to console, to solace, to enlighten, to perfect his neighbor. No person was better acquainted than he with the highest perfection; but he repeated himself for the little, and never disdained anything, however small. He made himself all to all, not to please all, but to gain all, and to gain them to Jesus Christ, not to himself."

To this judgment of the pious Bishop of Cambray we shall add that of the learned Bourdaloue: "The doctrine of St. Francis de Sales is a food, not of earth, but of Heaven, which, from the same substance, nourishes, like the manna, all kinds of persons; and I am able to say, without offending against the respect which I owe to all other writers, that after the Holy Scriptures there are no works that have better maintained piety among the faithful than those of this holy bishop."

The illustrious Monsignore of Paris shared the same

sentiments. "All that can contribute," he says, "to make the most amiable of saints better known to the world must be useful to the cause of our holy religion."

Thus, the three men who were the glory of the clergy of France in the age of Louis XIV were unanimous in esteeming and praising the works of this great master of the spiritual life.

Protestants themselves are obliged to render justice to the exceptional merit of the works of St. Francis de Sales. One of their best authors[2] thus appreciates the writings of the blessed Bishop of Geneva: "From its first appearance, the *Introduction to a Devout Life* had a universal success in France, and editions succeeded one another rapidly. This was an event of great consequence in regard to such a book, and Catholicism could most justly rejoice at it. The learned controversies of Bellarmine had been of far less advantage: they had indeed fitted for theological discussion a clergy who found themselves face to face with superior forces; but from the first blow, the *Introduction* could make conquests to a religion whose practices were presented under forms so amiable, and even so delightful. . . . Among Calvinistic gentlemen solicited to abjure their faith, the little book served as an occasion for more than one renunciation. In this respect, the *Introduction to a Devout Life* was, in the beginning of the century, what the *Exposition of the Catholic Faith* was in the middle, and had effects quite similar. Of all that St. Francis de Sales has written, his *Letters* are the most widely spread: Protestants read them after a selection,

---

2 *History of French Literature,* by M. Sayous.

for all would not suit their taste; but in each class, the amiable and glowing piety, the grace—what shall I say? the wit, the familiar gossip, with which the Bishop allows his pen to twirl along, have a singular charm; and never does the afflicted or dejected heart disdain the consolation and encouragement which it finds in perusing them."

It is in his correspondence that we must study the great, the holy Bishop of Geneva; there we shall find humility unparalleled, a joyous cordiality, peace unutterable, the sole desire of accomplishing the will of God.

There we shall find that elegance, ever new, in thought and in expression; that richness of beautiful images and of fine comparisons borrowed from things most familiar: the rose, the pigeon, the halcyon, the bee, the odorous plants of Arabia; that dovelike simplicity, that childlike candor which does not, however, exclude, on due occasions, a manly strength and energy; that chaste tenderness which could only come from Heaven; that gentle meekness which holds the key of every heart.

We shall be the less surprised at the eulogies given to the writings of St. Francis de Sales by the most experienced doctors and the most eminent personages, when we consider with what maturity and wisdom they were composed. Those beautiful pages, which seem to flow as from a well, so free and natural are the doctrine and the style, are the fruit of the most serious study and the most assiduous meditation, joined with a great knowledge of the human heart, which he had acquired in the direction of souls.[3]

---

3 *Spirit of St. Francis de Sales.*

His beautiful *Treatise on the Love of God* is the result of twenty-four years' preaching, according to the statement of the author himself, and the fruit of such profound study, that there are fourteen lines in it, which, as he told Mgr. Camus, Bishop of Belley, had cost him the reading of more than twelve hundred pages in folio.[4] After this, we should not be surprised at the unexampled success which has crowned the writings of St. Francis de Sales. The *Treatise on the Love of God* is a most beautiful book, and one that has had a great circulation. All the agitations, all the inconsistencies of the human heart are painted in it with inimitable art. We behold there the exercises of love, contemplation, the repose of the soul in God, its languors, its transports, its dereliction, its dying sadness, its return to courage, the abandonment of the docile spirit to the secret ways of Providence. When the *Introduction to a Devout Life* appeared in the world, it created an extraordinary sensation; everyone wished to procure it, to read it, and, having read it, to read it again. Very soon it was translated into nearly all the languages of Europe, and editions succeeded one another so rapidly that in 1656 it had reached the fortieth. Henry IV, on reading it, declared that the work far surpassed his expectations; Mary of Medici, his wife, sent it bound in diamonds and precious stones to James, King of England; and this monarch, one of the most learned who ever occupied a throne, conceived such an esteem for it, that, notwithstanding his schismatical and spiteful prejudices against Catholic

---

4   It is related that the publisher, in gratitude for the considerable gain he had derived from the sale of the *Introduction to a Devout Life,* made a journey to Annecy expressly to offer as a gift to the author a sum of four hundred crowns of gold. *(Memoirs of the Academic Society of Savoy,* Vol. II).

writers, he carried it always about with him and often read it. Many times he was heard to say: "Oh, how I should wish to know the author! He is certainly a great man, and among all our bishops there is not one capable of writing in this manner, which breathes of Heaven and the angels." The general of the Feuillants, speaking of this work, calls it the most perfect book that mortal hand ever composed, a book that one would always wish to read again after having read it many times, and he adds this beautiful eulogium, that in reading it he who would not be a Christian should become better, and he who would be better should become perfect.[5]

The Church, directed by the Holy Spirit, exhorts all her children to be guided by the counsels of St. Francis de Sales. *Admonished by his directions,* she says in his Office. She assures us that his works have diffused a bright light amongst the faithful, to whom they point out a way as sure as it is easy, to arrive at perfection.

We could, if our design permitted it, multiply evidence in favor of the works of St. Francis de Sales. We shall terminate this introduction by some extracts from a letter of Pope Alexander VII, one of the greatest of his panegyrists: "I conjure you anew to make the works of M. de Sales your delight and your dearest study. I have read them I cannot tell how many times, and I would not dispense myself from reading them again; they never lose the charm of novelty; they always seem to me to say something more than they had said before. If you trust me, these writings should be the mirror of your life, and the rule by which to form your

---

5 *Life of St. Francis de Sales,* by M. the Abbé Hamon.

every action and your every thought. As for me, I confess to you that from often reading them I have become like a repository of his most beautiful sentiments and the principal points of his doctrine, that I ruminate over them at my leisure, that I taste them, and that I make them, so to speak, pass into my very blood and substance. Such is my opinion of this great saint, exhorting you with all my heart to follow him."

If in gathering these lovely flowers and binding them into bunches, we have lessened their beauty or their perfume, we trust that still they will at least a little serve those severely tried souls for whom we intend them; we shall consider it an ample recompense for all our trouble, if, even in a single heart, they increase confidence in God, and the desire to love and serve Him generously.

"Most holy Mother of God, the most lovable, the most loving, and the most loved, of creatures! Prostrate at thy feet, I dedicate and consecrate to thee this little work of love, in honor of the immense greatness of thy love. O Jesus! To whom could I more fitly offer these words of Thy love than to the most amiable heart of the well-beloved of Thy soul?"[6]

---

6   Dedication of the *Treatise on the Love of God,* by St. Francis de Sales.

—Second Book—

Consoling Thoughts on Trials of an Interior Life,
Infirmities of Soul and Body, etc.

Chapter One

Maxims for Perseverance in Piety in the Midst of Afflictions

TO LIVE constantly in devotion, we have only to establish sound principles or maxims in our soul.

The first which I desire you to adopt is that of St. Paul: "All things work together for good to those who love God." And truly, since God is able and understands how to draw good from evil, for whom will He be disposed to do so, if not for those who give themselves unreservedly to Him? Even sins, which God in His goodness has forbidden, are changed by the Divine Providence to the good of those who belong to Him. David would not have been so full of humility if he had not sinned, nor Magdalen of love for her Saviour if He had not forgiven her many sins; and never would He have forgiven them, if she had not committed them.

Behold the great dispenser of mercy: He changes our

miseries into favors, and from the adder of our iniquities, makes a salutary balm for our souls. Tell me, then, I pray, what will He not do with our afflictions, our labors, our persecutions? If it happens that something grieves you, no matter from what quarter it comes, be assured that while you love God, all will turn to your good. And though you cannot see the means by which this good will come, be assured that it will come. If God places the bandage of ignominy over your eyes, it will be to render you an admirable sight, a spectacle of honor. If He permits you to fall, like St. Paul, whom He cast to the earth, it will be to raise you up with glory.

The second maxim is: that God is your Father; otherwise, He would not command you to say: Our Father, Who art in Heaven. And what have you to fear, being the child of such a Father, without whose Providence not a hair of your head can fall? It is wonderful that,[1] being the children of such a Father, we have, or could have, any other anxiety than to love and serve Him. Have the care He wishes you to have of yourself and your family, and no more; you will then see that He will have care of you. "Think of Me," He said to St. Catherine of Siena, "and I will think of thee." "O Eternal Father!" says the Wise Man, "Thy Providence directs all things."

Do not look forward to the occurrences of this life with fear, but accept them with perfect confidence that, as they happen, God will protect and deliver you; He has guarded you until the present; hold fast by the hand of His

---

1 "It is wonderful that"—that is, "It is a wonder that."—*Publisher,* 2013.

Providence, and He will assist you on all occasions: and where you cannot walk, He will carry you. What should you fear, belonging to God, who has so emphatically assured us, that *all things work together for good to those who love Him?*

The true servant of God is not solicitous about the morrow; he performs faithfully what God requires of him today, and will perform what God will require of him tomorrow, and the same the next day, and the next day, without a word. Thus he unites his will, not to the means of serving God, but to the service and good pleasure of God. "Be not solicitous about the morrow, and say not: What shall we eat? Or wherewith shall we be clothed? Or how shall we live? For your heavenly Father knoweth that you have need of all these things; seek first the Kingdom of God, and all these things shall be added unto you." (*Matt.* 6:31-33) This extends to spiritual, as well as to temporal things.

Remain in peace, remove from your imagination whatever can trouble it, and say frequently to Our Lord: *O God, Thou art my God, and I will confide in Thee; Thou wilt aid me, and be my refuge, and I shall fear nothing;* for Thou art not only with me, but Thou art in me, and I in Thee.

Your third maxim should be that which Our Lord taught His Apostles: Has anything been wanting to you? Our Lord had sent His Apostles to various places, without silver, without staff, without shoes, without scrip, with only one coat, and afterwards He said to them: When I sent you thus, was anything wanting to you? And they said: No. Still more, when you endured afflictions, even when you had little confidence in God, did you perish in those afflictions?

You will answer: No. And why, then, have you not courage to advance in spite of all other adversities? God has not abandoned you until the present; how will He abandon you henceforward, since now more than ever you desire to belong to Him?

Fear not evil to come upon you from this world; for, perhaps, such evil will never happen, and even if it should happen, God will strengthen you. He commanded St. Peter to walk upon the waves; and St. Peter, seeing the winds and the storm, was afraid; and fear sank him; he sought the assistance of his Master, who said: Man of little faith! Why didst thou doubt? And reaching out His hand, Our Lord helped him. If God requires you to walk on the waves of adversity, fear not, doubt not, God will be with you; have good courage and you shall be delivered.

The fourth maxim is: eternity. It matters little how these transitory moments pass, provided I enjoy eternally the glory of God. We advance into eternity, already we have one foot there; provided it be a happy eternity for us, what matter about these fleeting moments of pain? Are we aware that our tribulations of two or three days prepare for us innumerable eternal consolations, and yet shall we be unwilling to support them?

The fifth maxim is that of the Apostle: "God forbid that I should glory, except in the cross of my Jesus." Plant the cross of Jesus Christ crucified in your heart, and all the crosses of this world will appear to you as so many roses. Those who have once been pierced with the thorns of the crown of Our Lord, who is our head, can scarcely ever feel any other thorns.

I have noticed in doves that they mourn as they rejoice; that they sing the same air as well for their canticles of jubilation, as for those in which they plaintively lament their dolors; that whether joyful or sad, they never change their tune; it is always the same low rumbling murmur.

This is that holy evenness of mind which we should endeavor to possess; I do not say evenness of fancy, or of inclination, but of mind; for we need not make any account of the annoyances raised by the inferior part of our soul, whence all whims and inquietudes proceed, stirred up by the senses and passions, when the superior part of the soul does not perform its duty of being master, or when it does not keep good watch against the assaults and disturbances of its enemies, to make war upon them and subject them to its laws. I say that we must always remain firm and resolute in the superior part of our soul, for whose fidelity we make profession, and preserve a constant equanimity through favorable and unfavorable circumstances, in desolation as well as in consolation.

The holy man Job furnishes us with an example in point; for when God multiplied favors upon him, gave him children, and sent him everything he could desire in this life, he always returned the same thanks. What did he say but: Blessed be the name of the Lord? This was his canticle of love which he sang on every occasion. See him reduced to the extremity of affliction; how does he act? He sings his canticle of lamentation to the same air which he had used in the days of his joy. "We have received good things," he says "from the hand of the Lord: why should we not also receive evil things? The Lord gave me children and possessions; the Lord has taken them away: Blessed be the name of the Lord!" No other canticle at any time than: Blessed be the name of the Lord!

Oh, how like was this holy soul to the dove, which always rejoices and mourns in the same soft notes! Thus should we act; thus should we receive prosperity and adversity, consolations and afflictions, from the hand of the Lord, always singing the same sweet song: Blessed be the holy name of God! And to the air of an unchangeable equanimity.

Let us not act like those who weep when consolation is absent, and do nothing but sing when it has returned: in which they resemble certain animals, that grow morose and furious when the weather is wet and gloomy, but never cease to skip and gambol when it is beautiful and serene.

CHAPTER TWO

WHENCE OUR MISERIES COME

OUR first misery is that we esteem ourselves; if we fall into any sin or imperfection, we are astonished, troubled, impatient, simply because we thought there was something good, resolute, solid, within us; and, therefore, when we find that there was no such thing, we are grieved and offended at having deceived ourselves. If we knew ourselves as we really are, instead of being amazed to see ourselves prostrate on the ground, we should be surprised to see ourselves stand for a single day, or even for one hour.

Endeavor to perform your actions perfectly, and having done this, think no more about them; but think of what you have yet to do, advancing with simplicity in the way of God, without tormenting your mind. It is necessary to detest your defects, not with a detestation of trouble and vexation, but with a tranquil detestation, to behold them with patience, and to make them serve to lower you in your own esteem. Regard your faults with more compassion than indignation, more humility than severity, and preserve your heart full of a sweet, calm, peaceful love.

Our second misery is, that we love ourselves; if we have not sensible consolations, we are sad; if we meet with some difficulties in our just undertakings, we are filled with uneasiness to overcome them, because we are attached to our consolations, our comfort, and our convenience. We only wish for honey in the service of God, and do not look to Jesus prostrate on the earth, sweating blood through the effect of His interior desolation. We refuse to understand that as dry jams are the best, so the actions we perform in dryness are more meritorious in the sight of God than those which we perform in consolation.

God does not wish that we should enjoy the luxury of our faith, our hope, or our charity, unless an absolute necessity requires it; we possess those virtues, nevertheless, but we are like a child, deprived by its tutor of the management of its possessions. How happy we are to be thus weaned and deterred by our celestial Tutor! It is our duty to adore this amiable Providence, by casting ourselves into its arms. No, Lord! I do not wish for the enjoyment of my faith, my hope, or my charity, unless to say to Thee in truth, though without sensible satisfaction, that I would rather die than forsake my faith, my hope, or my charity. Lord! If it be Thy good pleasure that I experience no pleasure in the practice of virtue, I acquiesce therein with all my will.

Whenever any pain befalls us, we must receive it with

calm submission to the good pleasure of God. When any matter of joy happens to us, we must receive it peacefully, with moderation of mind, and without being too much elated.

CHAPTER THREE

CONDUCT TO BE OBSERVED IN INTERIOR TRIALS

IT IS an ordinary thing with those who begin to serve God, and who have not yet had experience of the withdrawal of grace, or of other spiritual vicissitudes, that as soon as they lose the feeling of sensible devotion, and the perception of that beautiful light which had invited them to run in the ways of God, they immediately lose breath, as it were, and fall into very great sadness and pusillanimity. Persons well versed in the matter give this explanation: they say that a reasonable being cannot remain for a long time famishing, and without any pleasure, heavenly or earthly; but as souls elevated above themselves by the taste of superior pleasures easily renounce all visible objects, so, when, by the divine appointment, this spiritual joy is taken away from them, they find they are also deprived of inferior consolations, and not being yet accustomed to await patiently the return of day, it seems to them that they are neither in Heaven nor on earth, but that they are to lie buried in a perpetual night; in such a manner that, like little children who have just been weaned, and who still seek their mother's breast, they can only weep and languish, being a trouble to everyone, but particularly to themselves.

Not to fall into discouragement, remark:

1. That God usually gives some foretaste of heavenly delights to those who enter into His service, in order to withdraw them from the pleasures of the world, and to encourage them in the pursuit of divine love: as a mother, to accustom her little infant to the breast, puts some honey there.

2. That, nevertheless, this good God, by an arrangement of His wisdom, sometimes takes away the milk and honey of His consolations, that we may learn to eat the dry and substantial bread of a severe devotion, practiced in the midst of disgusts and agitations.[1]

3. That great temptations often arise during times of aridity; when we must fight continually against the temptations, for they are not of God, but endure patiently the aridity, since He appoints it for our trial.

4. That we should never lose courage in the midst of interior pains, nor say: I shall never be joyful; for at night we should expect the light, and, on the other hand, at the brightest spiritual time, we should not say: I shall never be sad, for, as the Wise Man observes, in happy days we

---

1 "As for imperfect souls, to whom sensible consolations are not granted according to their desires, they trouble themselves unprofitably; perfection does not consist in those enjoyments, but in the love of God; and our reward will only be so much the greater, as we shall have acted in all things with more justice and truth."—*St. Teresa of Avila*

should remember the unhappy; we must hope in pain, and fear in prosperity; in both be humble.

5. I perceive that all the seasons of the year are to be found in your soul: sometimes winter, with sterility, distractions, torments, disgusts, and weariness; sometimes the roses of May, with the sweet scent of holy little flowers; sometimes the heats of desire to please our good God. There only remains autumn, when, as you say, you do not find much fruit; but it often happens that, in threshing the wheat and pressing the grapes, we find much more than the harvest and the vintage had promised. You would like always to have springtime or summer; but it is necessary to have a change internally, as well as externally. In Heaven there will be a perpetual spring as to beauty, a perpetual autumn as to joy, a perpetual summer as to love. There will be no winter there; but here winter is required for the exercise of self-denial, and for the growth of a thousand beautiful virtues which flourish only in sterility. Let us, then, make our little steps forward; if we have a good and resolute affection, we cannot but advance well. It is not necessary for the practice of virtues to be always attentive to them all. That would entangle and perplex your thoughts too much. Humility and charity are the antiphonarians; all the other virtues are annexed to them. The preservation of a house depends upon the foundation and the roof; if we attend to which, the rest will give us no great difficulty. Humility and charity are the mothers of virtues; the others follow them, as little chickens do the hens.

6. That it is a sovereign remedy, to discover our trouble to some wise friend who can solace us.

Finally, to conclude a warning that is necessary, I will remark that, in interior trials, as in all other things, our good God and our enemy have very different views. God makes use of these pains to guide us to great purity of heart, to an entire renunciation of our own interest in what concerns His service, and to a perfect stripping of ourselves; while the devil endeavors by these sufferings to make us lose courage, to make us return to sensual pleasures, and to make us wearisome both to ourselves and others, that holy devotion may be decried and defamed. But if you observe the instructions I have given you, you will greatly increase in perfection by the endurance of interior afflictions, of which, before concluding, I must say another little word. Sometimes disgusts, sterilities, and aridities proceed from indisposition of the body; as when by excessive watches, labors, and fasts, we are overwhelmed with fatigue, and weighed down by drowsiness, headache, and other such infirmities, which, though they depend on the body, do not fail to inconvenience the soul, on account of the strict union that exists between both. Yet, in this state, we should always be careful to elicit many acts of virtue, though in the summit of the soul, and with our superior will. For, though our soul is asleep, as it were, through weariness, that does not prevent the operations of our spirit from being most agreeable to God; and we may say to Him with the sacred spouse: "I sleep, but my heart watcheth." Lastly, if there is less pleasure in laboring thus, there is, as I have already said, more merit and virtue. As for the remedy, it is to strengthen the body by granting it some alleviation and fitting recreation. Thus St. Francis ordered his religious to moderate their labors in such a manner that fervor of spirit might not be impeded.

And, speaking of this glorious father, he was once attacked and agitated by so dreadful a melancholy, that he could not hinder it from appearing externally; for if he wished to converse with his religious, he could not; if he withdrew from them, he was still worse; abstinence and macerations reduced him to a shadow; prayer did not comfort him in the least. He remained in this state for two years, so that he seemed to be altogether abandoned by God. But at last, after humbly enduring this wild tempest, the Saviour restored to him, in one moment, a full and blessed tranquility. Thus, the greatest servants of God are subject to these rude shocks, and others should not be surprised if they sometimes get one too.

CHAPTER FOUR

PERPLEXITY OF THE HEART WHICH LOVES WITHOUT KNOWING WHETHER IT IS LOVED

IT SOMETIMES happens that we have no consolation in the exercises of holy love; so much so, that, like deaf religious, we can neither hear our voice in the choir, nor enjoy the sweetness of our chant; moreover, we are annoyed with a thousand fears, disturbed by a tremendous hurly-burly which the enemy raises round our heart, suggesting to us that perhaps we are not agreeable to our Master, and that our love is useless, or even false and vain, since it produces no consolation. We labor, then, not only without pleasure, but with extreme difficulty, seeing neither the good of our labor, nor any content that it can afford to Him for whom we labor.

But what increases the misery is, that the mind and reason cannot give us any kind of relief; for the superior part of the soul, being completely surrounded by the suggestions of the enemy, is in the greatest alarm, and is kept busy in guarding against being surprised by any consent to evil; so that it cannot make a sortie to set free the inferior part of the soul. And though it does not lose courage, yet it is so fiercely assaulted, that, if it is without blame, it is not without pain; for, to fill up the cup of its misfortune, it is deprived of that general consolation which accompanies nearly all the other afflictions of this world, namely, the hope that they will soon end; the heart, in these spiritual conflicts, falling into a kind of inability to think of their termination, and, consequently, being unconsoled by hope. Faith, indeed, residing in the summit of the soul, assures us that this trouble will end, and that we shall one day enjoy repose; but the terrific noise and shout, raised by the enemy throughout the inferior part of the soul, almost drown the voice of faith, with its warnings and encouragements; leaving only on the imagination this sad reflection: "I shall never be happy."

Alas, how afflicted is the poor heart, when it seems abandoned by love, which it seeks for everywhere, and cannot find! We do not find it in the exterior senses, for they are incapable of retaining it; nor in the imagination, which is cruelly tormented by a variety of impressions; nor in the reason, which is troubled with a thousand obscure lights and strange apprehensions; but at last we find it in the very summit of the soul, where it has all the while been residing; yet we do not recognize it, and it does not appear to be itself, because the greatness of the darkness and sorrow prevents us from perceiving its beauty. We see it without remembering it, and meet it without knowing it, as in a dream. Thus Magdalen, meeting her dear Master, did not derive any consolation from doing so, for she did not think it was He, but only the gardener.

Ah! What can the soul do, in this state? It knows not how to exist amid so many enemies, and has strength only to let its will die in the will of God, imitating the sweet Jesus, who, having arrived at the height of sufferings on the cross, which His Father had prepared for Him, did as the stag does, when, out of breath and overtaken by the hounds, it comes at last to bay, the tear in its eye. For thus the divine Saviour, approaching His death, and heaving His last sigh, with a loud cry and abundance of tears, said: "Father, into Thy hands I commend my spirit"; words which were His last, and by which the well-beloved Son gave the highest proof of His love to His Father. When, then, everything fails us, when our exhaustion is extreme, these words, this abandonment of our soul into the hands of our Saviour, cannot fail us. The Son recommends His spirit to His Father in His last and incomparable distress; and we, racked in the convulsions of interior pains, destitute of comfort, unable to live, surrender our spirit into the hands of the Eternal Son, who is our true Father, and, bowing down our head in acquiescence to His good pleasure, resign our whole will to Him.

Chapter Five

Means to Preserve Peace of Soul in Time of Trial

NOTHING disturbs us so much as self-love and self-esteem. If our heart does not overflow with tender emotions, if our mind does not teem with sublime sentiments, if our soul is not inundated with exquisite sweetness, we are sad; if anything difficult is to be done, if any obstacle opposes our just designs, behold us in a state of precipitation to have it overcome, and we are overcome ourselves by the precipitation. Why is this so? Undoubtedly, because we are too much attached to our comfort, our ease, our convenience. We would wish to say our prayers in a region of *eau de cologne,* and practice heroic virtue eating sugar cake; but we do not consider the *meek Jesus, prostrate on the earth, sweating blood,* through the dreadful combat that rages in His interior, between the feelings of the inferior part of His soul and the resolutions of the superior part.

Hence it happens that when we fall into any fault or sin, we are astonished, troubled, and impatient. We only desire consolations, and are unwilling to put a finger on our misery, our weakness, or our nothingness.[1]

Were we to do a few things, we should find peace: let us have a pure intention to seek on all occasions the honor and glory of God; let us perform the little we can for this object, according to the advice of our spiritual father, and leave the rest to God. Why should he who has God for the object of his intentions, and who does what he can, torment himself? Why should he trouble himself? What has he to fear? No, no, God is not so terrible to those who love Him; He is content with a little, for He knows that we have not much.

And know that Our Lord is called in Scripture the *Prince of Peace,* and hence, wherever He is absolute Master, He preserves peace. It is nevertheless true, that, before establishing peace in any place, He first makes war there, separating the heart and soul from their dearest and most intimate affections, such as immoderate love of oneself, confidence and complacency in oneself, and other like evils. When Our Lord separates us from these cherished and favorite passions, it seems as if He excoriated our living heart, and we are filled with the most bitter sentiments; we can hardly prevent our whole soul from discussing its misfortune, so sensible is this separation.

But all this disputation of mind is not inconsistent

---

1   "The sight of ourselves causes trouble, which is the just punishment of our self-love. "On the contrary, the sight of God gives peace, which is the recompense of pure love, and a foretaste of paradise."—*Fenelon.*

with peace, when, though almost submerged by desolation, we still keep our will resigned to that of Our Lord, nailed to His divine good pleasure, and cease not from the performance of our duties, but fulfill them courageously. Of which Our Lord gives us an example in the Garden; for, overwhelmed with interior and exterior affliction, He resigned His heart sweetly into His Father's will, saying: "Not my will, but Thine be done," and ceased not, great as was His anguish, to visit and admonish His disciples. To preserve peace in the midst of war, and sweetness in the midst of bitterness, is indeed worthy of the Prince of Peace.

From what I have just said, I desire you to draw three conclusions: first, that we often imagine peace to be lost, because we are in pain, while it is not lost, as may easily be known by the fact that we still wish to renounce ourselves, to depend on the good pleasure of God, and to fulfill the duties of our state; second, that we must of necessity endure interior pain, while God tears away the last remnant of the old man, to *renovate us in the new man who is created according to God,* and therefore we should not be troubled, or suppose that we have fallen into disgrace with Our Lord; third, that all those thoughts which cause vexation and agitation of mind cannot proceed from God, who is the Prince of Peace, but are temptations of the enemy, and therefore to be rejected and disregarded.

Humility enables us to view our imperfections undisturbed, remembering those of others. For why should we be more perfect than others? In like manner, it enables us to view the imperfections of others without trouble, remembering our own. For why should we think it strange that others have imperfections, when we have them ourselves? Humility makes our heart meek towards the perfect and the imperfect, towards the former through reverence, towards the latter through compassion. Humility helps us to receive sufferings meekly, knowing that we deserve them, and favors reverently, knowing that we do not deserve them. As to the exterior, I approve of your making every day some act of humility, either in word or deed: I mean by words coming from the heart, such as words humbling you to an inferior; in deed, as by performing some little office or service for the house or for individuals.

I would like you to read Chapter 41 of the *Way of Perfection* by the blessed mother, St. Teresa, for it will aid you to understand what I have so often said, that we must not cavil too much about the practice of virtues, but approach them valiantly, honestly, freely, in a *bona fide* way: I dread the unreasonably screwed-up spirit of restraint and melancholy. No, I desire you to have a great and generous heart in the service of Our Lord, yet to be humble, meek, and sincere.

For want of this, our imperfections, which we view so narrowly, trouble us much, and are thus retained; for nothing preserves them better than anxiety and uneasiness to remove them.

CHAPTER SIX

TO ATTAIN PERFECTION
WE MUST PATIENTLY ENDURE
OUR IMPERFECTION

THE feast of the Purification has no octave; it should
continue our whole life.

We must have our mind settled on two points: one,
to expect the growth of weeds in our garden; the other, to
have courage to witness their removal, and to lend a hand
ourselves. For self-love will not die as long as we live, and
it is the origin of all those unwelcome productions. Man
carries himself everywhere about with him, finds himself
everywhere, and misery is attached to him as a shadow to
the body.

According to the general opinion of good people, you
should suspect all those desires which cannot be followed
by their effects. Such are the desires of a certain Christian perfection which may be imagined, but cannot be

practiced, and of which many can give lessons, but none a specimen.

Know that the virtue of patience is that which secures us the greatest perfection; and if we must have patience with others, we must also have it with ourselves. Those who aspire to the pure love of God, have more need of patience with themselves than with others.

To attain perfection, we must endure our imperfection. I say: we must suffer it with patience, not love or cherish it; humility is fortified in suffering.

We must acknowledge the truth: we are miserable creatures, who can scarcely do any good; but God, who is infinitely good, is content with our little works, and the preparation of our heart is agreeable to Him. (*Psalm* 9:38).

To travel well, we should apply ourselves to the present day's journey, and not concern ourselves about the final one before we have finished the first. Remember this: we sometimes amuse ourselves so much about being good angels, that we hardly labor to become good men.

Our imperfection will accompany us to the grave. We cannot walk without touching the ground. It is not necessary to lie or wallow there; neither is it necessary to think of flying; for we are so small, that we have not yet got wings. We die little by little; so we must also die to our imperfections day by day. O precious imperfections! Which show us our misery, exercise us in humility and self-contempt, in patience and diligence, and in spite of which, God has regard to the preparation of our heart, that it may be perfect!

You complain of the many imperfections and defects to be found in your life, contrary to your desire of perfection, and to the purity of the love of God. I answer that anything else is impossible here below. We must carry ourselves about with us until God carries us to Heaven; and so long as we carry ourselves, we shall have nothing to boast of.

O God, how great a blessing it is to know our weakness and our misery! This knowledge will serve us for the remainder of our days. "What does he know," says the Holy Scripture, "who has not been tempted?" My God, how much I desire to be humbled and confounded![1]

Live joyful: Our Lord looks upon you, and looks upon you with love, and with tenderness in proportion to your weakness. Never permit your mind to willingly entertain thoughts to the contrary, and when they come, regard them not; turn your eyes away from their iniquity, and turn them towards God with a courageous humility, to speak to Him of His ineffable goodness, by which He loves our poor, abject, fallen nature, notwithstanding all its misery.

Our imperfections need not please us; we must say with the great Apostle: "Miserable man that I am! Who will deliver me from this body of death?" But they need not astonish us, or take away our courage; we should rather draw submission, humility, and diffidence in ourselves from them, but not discouragement, nor affliction of heart, much less doubtfulness of the love of God towards us. Thus God does not love our imperfections nor venial sins, but He loves us much notwithstanding them. As the weakness and infirmity of an infant displease its mother, yet she does not cease to love it, but loves it tenderly and compassionately;

---

1   Distrust over-anxious desires for good; they are full of self-love and of impatience *to be something.*

so God, while He does not approve of our imperfections or venial sins, ceases not to love us tenderly; wherefore, David could say with reason to Our Lord: "Have mercy on me, O Lord, for I am weak."

We must have patience, and not expect to cure in one day the many bad habits that we have contracted, through the little care we have taken of our spiritual health. God has indeed cured some persons speedily, in an instant, without a vestige of their malady remaining, as in the case of Magdalen, who, in a moment, was changed from a sink of corruption into a fountain of perfection, and was never afterwards troubled.

But this same God left, for a considerable time after their conversion, in many of His dear disciples, marks of their former inclinations: and all for their greater good: witness the blessed St. Peter, who, after his vocation, was often surprised by imperfections, and once fell miserably.[2]

Solomon makes mention of an animal as insolent as the servant who suddenly becomes mistress. There is great reason to fear that the soul which, for a long time, has served its passions and affections, would become proud and vain, if in a moment it were made perfect mistress of them. We must only acquire this ascendancy little by little, and step by step; it has engaged the saints for years and scores of years.

---

2   In order to obtain the remission of light faults, it is better, after having acknowledged them, to turn humbly and lovingly towards God, than to preserve a sad remembrance of them and to remain a long time in fear. Whether your prevarications be serious or trivial, remain in pious sentiments of confidence towards the Lord, casting your sins into the abyss of His mercy, that they may be forever lost there; for *there is no damnation to those who are in Jesus.*

We must, if we please, have patience with everyone, and particularly with ourselves. Have a little patience, and you will see that all will go well; for the dear Saviour of our souls has not given us those inflamed desires of serving Him, without intending to provide some opportunity for doing so. He postpones the hour of the accomplishment of your holy desires only to make you find it happier; for the loving Heart of our Redeemer arranges and adjusts the events of this world to the greater good of those who unreservedly devote themselves to His love. It will come then, the happy hour you desire, the day which Providence has named in the secrets of its mercy; and then, with a thousand consolations, you will unfold your interior before the divine goodness, the rocks will be changed into water, the serpent into a rod, and all the thorns of your heart into roses, sweet scented roses, to recreate your mind with their delicious perfume. It is true that our faults, which, while in the heart, are thorns, on coming forth by a voluntary accusation, are converted into roses; and as our malice raises them in the soul, so the goodness of the Holy Spirit drives them out.

There is nothing without trouble in this world; we must, therefore, compose our will in such a manner as not to seek for our convenience, or if we do seek for it, to accommodate ourselves to those inconveniences which are inseparably attached to every convenience. We have no wine without lees. We must then examine whether it is better to have thorns in our garden, while we have roses there, than to have no roses, so as to have no thorns.

I pray our sweet Saviour to pour His holy unction over you, that you may repose tranquilly and securely on Him.

O God! I recommend to Thee this poor heart of ours; comfort and strengthen it, that it may the better serve Thee; for such is the motive of our request. The heart is the lamb of holocaust which we must offer to God; it should always be in the best condition possible. It is the bed of the spouse; we should sprinkle it with flowers. Console then this poor heart, and give it an increase of joy and peace, that it may the better serve its Lord. Alas! What else have we to desire than this? Glory be to God! God or nothing; for all that is not God is nothing, or worse than nothing.

Let us always keep walking; though we advance slowly, yet we shall make much way. Your weakness, you say, impedes your progress, for it hinders you from entering into yourself, or approaching to God. This is certainly speaking ill. God leaves you thus for His glory and for your greater advantage. He wishes your misery to become the throne of His mercy, and your impotence to be the seat of His omnipotence. Where did God place the divine strength of Samson, unless in his hair, the very weakest part of him? Let no one blame her who would wish to serve God according to His holy pleasure, and not according to sensible consolations.

Beware of falling into any kind of distrust; for the celestial goodness does not permit you to meet with those falls in order to abandon you, but to humble you, and to make you hold more firmly by the hand of God's mercy.

You please me exceedingly by continuing your exercises in the midst of the aridities and interior languors which have seized on your soul. For since we wish to serve God only for love, and the services we render to Him, in the midst of aridity, are more acceptable to Him than those performed in the flow of consolation, we should also, on our part, endeavor to be more attached to them, at least with our superior will; and though, according to self-love, tenderness may be sweeter, yet, according to the views of God, dryness may be more profitable, as dry meats are more useful to dropsical persons than moist ones, though they prefer the latter.

Never permit your mind to think too much on its miseries; leave them to God; He will do something with them. Hardly bestow a thought on the share self-love has in these considerations; its sallies are to be neglected; to disown them two or three times a day is sufficient. We must not push them out with strength of arm, but merely say one little: "No."

Have great courage, and take a long breath. Our enemy is a great clamorer; you need not be disturbed, for he cannot hurt you; laugh at him, and let him go; this treatment completely kills him. He has often bawled around the saints with a wonderful hubbub; but what came of it, unless that they are now at rest in the place which he, miserable wretch, lost?

CHAPTER SEVEN

WE MUST LABOR AT OUR PERFECTION WITHOUT UNEASINESS

THERE are two very different chords, yet equally necessary to be tuned, before playing on the lute, namely, the treble and the bass. It would seem, at first sight, that nothing could be more discordant than a high note and a low note; yet, by their harmony, the most agreeable music is produced, and, in the absence of either, the lute would be unattractive. In like manner, on our spiritual lute, there are two things naturally contrary, and of necessity to be tuned, before evoking any sweet sounds: these are, to have a great care of perfecting ourselves, and to have no care of our perfection, but to leave it entirely to God; I mean to say that we must have the care which God wishes us to have of perfecting ourselves, and, nevertheless, leave to Him the care of our perfection. God wishes us to have a peaceful and tranquil care, such as will make us perform what is judged proper by those who guide us, and that we go faithfully forward in the way marked out by the rules and directions given us; as for the rest, to repose on His paternal bosom, endeavoring, as far as possible, to keep our soul at peace; for the abode of God is in Himself and in the peaceful heart. You know that on a serene night, when the lake is calm, its waters unrippled by a breath of wind, the sky is so well shadowed in it, with all the stars, that, looking down, we see the beauty of the heavens there as well as if we raised our eyes on high. In like manner, when our soul is tranquil, unagitated by the winds of superfluous care, unevenness of disposition, or inconstancy of mind, it is well suited to bear an image of Our Lord. But when it is troubled and disquieted by divers gusts and squalls of passions, and we allow ourselves to be blown about by them, and are not governed by reason, which makes us like to God, we are then incapable of representing in ourselves the beautiful and holy image of Our Crucified Lord, or the diversity of His excellent virtues, or of presenting our soul as a nuptial bed worthy of Him. We must, then, leave the care of ourselves to the mercy of Divine Providence, and, nevertheless, do plainly and simply what lies in our power to amend and perfect ourselves, always taking the greatest care not to trouble or disquiet our souls.

There is no weariness so weary as that which arises from the annoyance of many little but pressing and continual importunities. Our Lord sometimes permits us to fall short in those little encounters, that we may be humbled, and learn that if we have at any time surmounted great temptations, it was not by our own strength we did so, but by the assistance of His divine goodness.

Do not waste time in combating the temptations that happen to you, by contests and disputes with them; only cast some simple glances of love towards Jesus Christ crucified, as if you would wish to kiss His sacred side or feet.

Cast many times a day your whole heart, mind, and care on God, with the utmost confidence, saying to Him, in the words of David: "I am Thine, O Lord; save me."

Live entirely for God, and for the love He has borne to you, endure yourself with all your miseries.

I do not mean to say by this, that you should continually be tying up your mind in order to hold it in peace; for you must do everything with the simplicity of a loving heart, keeping near Our Lord as a little child near its father, and when you happen to fall into some faults, whatever they may be, ask pardon meekly, saying to Him that you are certain He loves you well, and will forgive you, and this always simply and sweetly.

All the ancient religious were most admirable in the confidence which they possessed that God would always give them whatever they should require for the support of life; but I consider that we ought to repose on Divine Providence, not only for what concerns temporal things, but much more for what relates to our spiritual life and perfection. It is only the too great care we have of ourselves that makes us lose our tranquility of mind, and leads us to odd and fantastic notions; for when we meet with some contradiction, and perceive a little of our immortification, or when we commit some fault, however trifling it may be, we immediately imagine that all is lost. Is it so great a wonder then to see you stumble occasionally? "But I am so miserable, so full of imperfections!" Are you well aware thereof? Bless God for having given you this knowledge, and do not lament it so much; you are very lucky in knowing that you are only misery itself. After having blessed God for the knowledge He has given you, remove that useless tenderness which makes you mourn over your infirmities. We have some sympathies for our body that are very much opposed to perfection, and others for our soul that are incomparably more so. "I am unfaithful to Our Lord, and therefore I have no consolation in prayer." A great pity indeed! "But I am so often in aridity, that it makes me believe I am not well with God, who is so full of consolations!" Capitally said, as if God always gave consolations to His friends! Was there ever a pure creature so worthy of being loved by God, and in reality so loved by Him, as Our Lady or St. Joseph? And yet sorely they were tried!

In a word, be not vexed, because you have been vexed; nor troubled, because you have been troubled; nor disquieted, because you have been disquieted by those annoying passions; but resume control over your heart, and place it lovingly in the hands of Our Lord, begging of Him to heal it: on your part, doing as much as you can for this purpose, by the renovation of your resolutions, perusal of good books, and other such means; and acting thus, you will gain considerably by your loss, and become much healthier by your sickness.

At the birth of Jesus, while the shepherds enjoyed celestial music and a glorious heavenly vision, Mary and Joseph in the stable beheld only the tears of the Divine Infant through the obscurity of the night. Yet who would prefer the condition of the former to that of the latter? Or who would not prefer to be with Jesus, Mary, and Joseph, though in the darkness of obscurity, than to be enraptured with the shepherds, though their joys were angelic?

CHAPTER EIGHT

INDIFFERENCE ABOUT OUR ADVANCEMENT IN VIRTUE

GOD has ordered us to do everything we can for the acquirement of holy virtues; let us, then, neglect nothing to succeed in this holy enterprise. But after we have "planted and watered," let us know that it is God who "gives increase" to the plants of our good habits and inclinations. We must, therefore, expect the fruit of our desires and labors from Divine Providence. And if we do not perceive the progress and advancement of our souls in a devout life to be such as we could wish, let us not be troubled, let us remain in peace, let tranquility ever dwell in our hearts. It is for us to cultivate carefully our souls, and so far we must be faithfully attentive. But as for the abundance of the harvest, let us leave the care of that to Our Lord. The laborer cannot be blamed if a splendid crop is wanting, but deservedly if he has neglected to till the ground and sow the seed.

Let us not be disturbed to find ourselves always novices in the practice of virtue; for, in the convent of a devout life, everyone considers himself always a novice, and the whole life there is destined to probation, no evidence being more convincing that one is not only a novice, but even deserving of expulsion and reprobation, than to imagine himself professed; for according to the rules of this order, it is not by the solemnity, but by the accomplishment of vows, that novices are professed. Now vows are never accomplished, so long as anything remains to be done for their observance, and the obligation of serving God and of making progress in His love endures until death. "But," someone will say to me, "suppose I know that it is by my own fault my advancement in virtue is retarded, how can I prevent myself from being saddened and disquieted?" It is necessary to be sorry for faults committed, with a repentance, strong, calm, peaceful, and constant, not turbulent, not disheartened. Are you certain that your delay on the highway of virtue is the result of your own fault? If so, humble yourself before God, implore His mercy, entreat His forgiveness, confess your fault, and cry to Him for mercy, even in the ear of your confessor, to obtain absolution for it. But having done this, remain in peace, and having detested the offence, embrace lovingly the disquiet that is left to you for the delay of your advancement in good. Behold this beautiful soul, I beg of you: it greatly desired and strove to get free from anger, in which God favored it, for He discharged it from all the sins that had previously proceeded from anger; it would now wish to die rather than say a single injurious word, or allow one sign of hatred to escape it. Nevertheless, it is still subject to the assaults and first movements of this passion, which are certain starts, shocks, and sallies of an irritated heart, that the Chaldaic paraphrase terms tremblings or flutterings, saying: "Tremble, and sin not," where our sacred version has it: "Be angry, and sin not"; which is in fact the same thing; for the prophet only means to say, that if anger surprises us, exciting in our hearts those first flutterings, we must take care not to allow ourselves to be carried further, or we shall commit "sin." But though these tremblings are no sin, yet the poor afflicted soul is often troubled and disquieted by them, and thinks it does well to be sad, as if it were the love of God that could produce this sadness. Heavenly love does not produce this sadness, for it is offended only with sin; it is our self-love, which would have us exempt from the pain and labor attached to those assaults. It is not the fault that displeases us in those bursts of anger, for there is no sin therein; it is the pain of resisting them that annoys us.

The rebellions of the sensual appetite, in regard to anger as well as to concupiscence, are left in us for our exercise, that we may display spiritual valor in overcoming them. This appetite is the Philistine whom the true Israelite must ever combat, without ever conquering; we may weaken him, but cannot destroy him. He dies only with us, and lives as long as we live. He is, indeed, an execrable and detestable enemy, being the fruit of sin, and tending only to sin. On which account, as we are called "dust," because taken from the earth and returning to the earth, so this rebellion is called "sin" by the great Apostle, because it comes from sin and leads to sin, though it does not render us guilty of sin, unless we obey it. Whence the same Apostle warns us to act in such a manner that this evil "may not reign in our mortal body, to obey its concupiscence." It is not to feel sin, but to consent to sin, he forbids; he does not order us to prevent sin from entering into us, and being there, but he commands that it shall not "reign" there. It is in us when we perceive the rebellion of the sensual soul; but it does not reign in us, unless we consent to its dominion.

"The sting of the flesh," "the angel of Satan," roughly tried the great St. Paul, to precipitate him into sin. The poor Apostle suffered it as a shameful and infamous injury; wherefore, he called it a "buffeting," and besought God to be pleased to deliver him from it; but God answered him: "O Paul! My grace is sufficient for thee, for My power is made perfect in infirmity." To which this great saint, acquiescing, said: "Then willingly will I glory in my infirmities, that the power of Jesus Christ may dwell in me." But, if you please, remark that the sensual rebellion is found even in this admirable vessel of election, who, by having recourse to the remedy of prayer, teaches us the means of overcoming the temptations we experience; remark also, that if Our Lord permits those cruel revolts in man, it is not always to punish him for some sin, but it is to manifest the power and energy of the divine grace and assistance; remark, in fine, that we should not only be untroubled about our temptations and infirmities, but should even glory in them, that the divine strength may appear in us, supporting our frailty against the attacks and suggestions of temptation. For the glorious Apostle calls the stings and darts of impurity which he felt, his infirmities, and says that he gloried in them, because if by his misery he endured them, yet, by the mercy of God, he did not consent to them.

God wishes that we should have enemies; God wishes that we should repel them. Let us, then, live courageously in the accomplishment of the divine will, suffering with patience to be assaulted, and with bravery resisting the assaults.

Chapter Nine

We Should Draw Profit from Our Faults

THE faults and infidelities of which we are guilty every day should indeed bring us shame and confusion, when we approach Our Lord; and thus we read of great saints, like St. Catherine of Siena, and St. Teresa, that, when they had fallen into any fault, they experienced much confusion.[1] Hence it is very reasonable, that, having offended God, we should retire from Him for a little by humility, and remain confused; for if we had offended only a friend, we should be ashamed to go near him.

But we must not remain away always; for the virtues of humility, abjection, and confusion are medium virtues, through which we must ascend to the union of our soul with God. It would be no great matter to annihilate and confound oneself, which is done by an act of humiliation,

---

1 Confusion—humiliation, embarrassment.—*Publisher,* 2013.

if it were not to give oneself to God, as St. Paul teaches us when he says: "Divest yourselves of the old man, and put on the new." For we are not to remain naked, but to clothe ourselves with God. This little retirement is made only the better to rush into God by an act of love and confidence. We must not confound sadness with inquietude: it is self-love that raises a good deal of this confusion, because we are offended at not being perfect, less through love for God than love for ourselves; and though you do not feel confidence, you should not cease to make acts thereof, saying to Our Lord: My Lord! Though I have no sentiment of confidence in Thee, yet I know that Thou art my God, I am all Thine, and I have no hope but in Thy goodness; hence I abandon myself entirely into Thy hands.

It is always in our power to make these acts, and though we may have some difficulty, yet there is no impossibility in the way, and it is on such occasions that we show our fidelity to Our Lord; for though we make them without relish or satisfaction, still we have no need to be in pain on that account, since Our Lord prefers them so: and do not say that you utter them only from the mouth; for if the heart did not wish it, the mouth would not say a word. Having acted thus, remain in peace, and without attending to your trouble, speak to Our Lord of something else. To conclude this point, it is good to have confusion, when we have a knowledge and feeling of our misery and imperfection; but we must not rest there, or fall therefrom into discouragement, but lift our heart to God by a holy confidence, the foundation of which should be in Him, and not in ourselves, inasmuch as we change, but He never changes:

always remaining the same, and as good and merciful when we are weak and imperfect, as when we are strong and perfect. I am accustomed to say that our misery is the throne of God's mercy; we must, therefore, as our misery is great, have so much the greater confidence.

To be a good servant of God is not to be always consoled, always in sweetness, always without aversion or repugnance for virtue; if it were, then neither St. Paul, nor St. Angela, nor St. Catherine of Siena, would have properly served God. To be a good servant of God is to be charitable towards our neighbor, to possess an inviolable resolution in the superior part of the soul to follow the will of God, to have such a profound humility and simplicity as will make us confide entirely in God and rise again when we fall, to endure patiently ourselves and our abjections, and to endure tranquilly our neighbors and their imperfections.

Certainly, when we take occasion from the sight of our imperfections to become humble, we gain considerably by our loss; inasmuch as the profit we make by advancing in the excellent virtue of humility is a rich reparation for the damage sustained by our frailty.

CHAPTER TEN

ADVANTAGES WHICH WE SHOULD DRAW FROM OUR DEFECTS

THE matter on which I am about to treat is one of the most important of a spiritual life. It is certain that, in the views of God, the faults into which He permits us to fall should serve for our sanctification, and that it depends on ourselves to draw this advantage from them.

What I have to say on this subject does not concern those cowardly and selfish souls, who make reservations with God, and who wish only to belong to Him to a certain degree. They commit, with foresight and reflection, a thousand faults, from which it is impossible they should derive any advantage, considering their evil dispositions. The persons for whom I write are those only who are determined not to commit any fault deliberately, though many escape them through surprise, inadvertence, and weakness, notwithstanding their resolution.

It usually happens that such persons are astonished and troubled at their faults, conceive a false shame for them, and fall into vexation and discouragement. These are the effects of self-love, and are much more pernicious than the faults themselves. We are surprised at falling: an evident mark that we scarcely know ourselves. We ought, on the contrary, to be surprised at not falling more frequently, and into more grievous faults, and to return thanks to God for the dangers from which He preserves us. We are troubled every time that we are beguiled into some fault, lose interior peace, are agitated, and spend hours, even days, thinking of it. We should never be troubled; but when we find ourselves on the ground, arise tranquilly, return to God with love, ask His forgiveness, and reflect no more on what has occurred, unless when it is necessary to accuse ourselves of it. We have a false shame for our faults; we call hardly venture to discover them to our confessor. "What idea will he have of me after so many promises, so many assurances, I have given him?" If you declare your faults simply and humbly, he will have more esteem for you. If you have a difficulty in telling them to him, his confidence in you will diminish on account of your want of sincerity. But the worst of all is that we are vexed at being vexed, and impatient at being impatient. What a misery! Should we not see that this is pride, that we are humbled on finding ourselves less holy than we had imagined, that we aspire to be exempt from imperfections and faults only in order to applaud and congratulate ourselves on having spent one day or week without much matter of reproach? In fine, we are discouraged; we abandon our exercises one by one; we give up prayer;

we regard perfection as impossible, and despair of arriving at any such height. What will this constraint, we say, this continual watching over oneself, this struggle after recollection and mortification, avail us, since we correct nothing, fall incessantly, and never become better? There is not a craftier snare of the demon than this. Would you wish to be protected from it? Never be discouraged, and no matter what fault you happen to commit, say: Though I should fall twenty times, or a hundred times, a day, I will arise at every fall, and pursue my course. What does it amount to, after all, that you should have met with some accidents on the way, provided you safely reach the journey's end? God will not reproach you after your recovery. Very often those mishaps proceed from the rapidity of our speed, and from that ardor which prevents us from taking the necessary precautions. Timid and cautious souls, who always wish to see where they put their foot, who turn aside every moment for fear of making a false step, who cannot bear to have their shoes soiled, never advance so quickly as others, who are less punctilious, but more daring, and whom death often overtakes in the midst of their course. It is not those who commit the least number of faults who are the most holy, but those who have the greatest courage, the greatest generosity, the greatest love, who make the boldest efforts to overcome themselves, and are not immoderately apprehensive of tripping, or even of falling and being dirtied a little, provided they advance.

St. Paul has told us that everything turns to good for those who love God. Everything turns to their welfare, even their faults, and sometimes the most grievous faults. God permits those faults in order to heal a vain presumption, and to teach us what we are, and of what we are capable. David acknowledged that the adultery and homicide into which he had fallen served to keep him in continual distrust of himself. "It is a blessing for me," he says to God, "That Thou hast humbled me; I have been more faithful since to Thy commandments." The fall of St. Peter was a most useful lesson to him, and the humility with which it inspired him disposed him to receive the gifts of the Holy Ghost, and to become head of the Church, and preserved him amid the dangers of so eminent a position. St. Paul, during the period of his greatest success in the apostleship, preserved himself against pride and vanity, by remembering that he had been a blasphemer and a persecutor of the Church of God. A humiliating temptation, from which God would not deliver him, served as a counterpoise to the sublimity of his revelations.

If God knows how to draw advantage even from the greatest sins, who can suppose that He will fail to turn our daily faults to our sanctification? It is a remark made by the masters of a spiritual life, that very often God leaves in the holiest souls some defects, which, notwithstanding all their endeavors, they cannot eradicate. He acts thus in order to make them feel their weakness; to show them what they would be without grace, to guard them from the inflation of vanity on account of His favors, to dispose them to receive other benefits with greater humility, to keep a holy self-hatred alive in their breasts, to withdraw them from the snares of self-love, to preserve their fervor and confidence towards Him, and to teach them the necessity of having continual recourse to prayer. The child that tumbles when it wanders a little distance from its mother, returns to her with greater tenderness, and from experience learns not to quit her in a hurry again. The lesson it has received on its own weakness and its mother's goodness, inspires it with a livelier affection for her.

The faults into which we fall often give place to great acts of virtue, which, otherwise, we should never have had occasion to practice, and God permits our faults for this end. For example, a dash of temper, a brusque reply, a manifest impatience, just fits one for a good act of humility, which abundantly repairs the fault and the scandal it had given. The fault is committed by a sudden impulse; the reparation is made with reflection, by a victory over oneself, and with a full and deliberate will. The latter is an act much more agreeable to God, than the former as a fault was disagreeable to Him.

God makes use of our faults and apparent imperfections to conceal our sanctity from the eyes of others, and to procure us humiliations from them.

God is a great master; let us allow Him to act. He will not fail at His work. Let us propose to ourselves to avoid carefully the least thing in the world that could displease Him. But when we shall have fallen into some faults, let us be sorry on His account, not on our own, let us cherish the abjection arising from our mishaps, and constantly beg of God to draw from them His own glory and our humiliation. He will do so, and advance us a great deal further by this means than by a life more regular and holy in appearance, but not so efficacious for the destruction of self-love.

When God requires certain things from us, let us not retire under pretext of the faults we should commit in performing them. It is much better to do good with imperfection, than to omit it. Sometimes we do not give a correction that is necessary, through fear of being carried away by impatience. We avoid the conversation of certain persons whose faults offend and annoy us. But how shall we acquire virtues, if we fly their occasions? Is not this a greater fault than that into which we fear to fall? Let us have a good intention, attend where duty calls, and be satisfied that God is sufficiently indulgent to pardon us the faults into which His service and our desire of pleasing Him expose us.

CHAPTER ELEVEN

_____

TRIALS IN PRAYER

PRAYER illumines our understanding with a divine light, and lays open our will to the holy flames of celestial love. Nothing so much purifies our mind from its errors, or our will from its depraved affections. It is a water of benediction, which makes the plants of our good desires grow green again and flourish, satiates the thirst of our hearts, and allays the heat of irregular concupiscence.

That uneasiness you experience at prayer, and which is joined with a great anxiety to discover some object capable of arresting and contenting your mind, is alone sufficient to prevent you from finding what you seek. When we search for anything with too much eagerness, we pass it by a hundred times without perceiving it.

The result of this vain and useless anxiety is weariness of mind; hence, coldness and torpor of soul. I know not what remedies you should use, but if you can possibly prevent this solicitude, you will do a good work; devotion cannot meet a more pestiferous enemy. It takes the semblance of endeavoring to excite us towards virtue, but only in order to cool us; and makes us run, but to overthrow us. We must, then, guard against excessive ardor on all occasions, but particularly in prayer.

To assist you in this, you should remember that the graces and favors of prayer are not earthly, but heavenly waters, which all our efforts cannot acquire, but for which indeed we must dispose ourselves with humble and tranquil care.

We must hold up our heart open to Heaven, and await the sacred dew. And never forget to carry this consideration to prayer, that therein we approach to God, and do so for two principal reasons.

The first is to render to God the honor and homage which we owe Him, and this can be done without His speaking to us, or our speaking to Him; acknowledging by our presence that He is our God, and we His vile creatures, and remaining prostrate in spirit before Him, awaiting His commands.

How many courtiers are there who appear a hundred times before the king, not to speak to him, or hear him, but simply to be seen by him, and to testify by their assiduity that they are his servants! This motive of presenting ourselves before God merely to attest our engagement in His service is most pure, worthy, and excellent, and, consequently, of the highest perfection.

The second reason for which we come before God is to speak to Him, and to hear Him speak to us by His inspirations and interior motions, and this is usually performed with a delicious pleasure, because it is a great happiness to speak to so mighty a Lord, and when He answers, He is accustomed to pour out such precious balm and unction as fill the soul to overflowing with sweetness.

One of these reasons may sometimes fail us, but both never. If we can speak to Our Lord, let us speak to Him, praise Him, beseech Him, listen to Him; if we cannot, because we are hoarse, let us remain in His chamber, and pay Him reverence; He will observe us there, regard our patience, and be pleased with our silence. Another time we shall be amazed when He takes us by the hand, and shows us everything, making a hundred turns along the beautiful walks of the garden of prayer; but even if He should never do so, we ought to be content with fulfilling our duty of accompanying His suite, and consider that it is already too great an honor for Him to endure us in His presence.[1]

Put aside those heartrending inquietudes, and no longer say that you can do nothing in prayer. What would you wish to do there, but what you really do, which is, to represent and offer to God your misery and nothingness? The most beautiful address that beggars make, is to expose to our eyes their sores and their rags.

But sometimes, you will tell me, you cannot even do

---

1 "A soul should not resolve, on account of the drynesses it experiences, to abandon prayer, even though its trials continue always; it should regard them as a very profitable cross to carry in the footsteps of its Saviour, who invisibly assists it. We cannot lose anything in the company of so good a Master, and the time will come when He will repay, with interest, our fidelity. Our Lord permits these and such like pains to happen to some persons in the beginning, and to others during the course of their exercises in prayer. The graces with which He intends to honor us at last being so great, He wishes first of all to make us understand how vast is our misery, that we may be preserved from pride."—*St. Teresa of Avila.*

so much as this, for you remain there as a shadow or a statue. Very well; that is just as good. In the palaces of kings there are statues arranged, which serve only to recreate the royal vision. Be content, then, as one of these in the presence of God. He will animate this statue when He pleases.

You ask me how you should act in order to carry your soul straight to God, without looking to the right hand or to the left.

The question is so much the more agreeable to me, as it carries its answer along with it. You must do what you say, go straight to God, without looking to the right hand or to the left.

This is not what you ask, I see, but how you should act in order so to establish your soul on God, that nothing may be able to detach it from Him.

Two things are necessary for that, namely, to die and to be saved; no more separation then; but your soul will be indissolubly attached and united to its God.

You say that this is not yet what you ask, but how you should act in order to prevent the least trifle from withdrawing your soul from God, as only too often happens.

You mean to say, I suppose, the least distraction; well, you ought to know that the least trifle of a distraction cannot withdraw your soul from God, since nothing withdraws us from God but sin, and the resolution we make in the morning to keep our soul united to God, and attentive to His presence, has the effect of preserving us thus always, even when we sleep, since we do all in the name of God, and according to His most holy will.

Even venial sins are not capable of turning us aside

from the way which conducts to God; they undoubtedly retard us a little on our course, but they do not turn us aside: much less simple distractions.

So far as prayer is concerned, it is not less useful, or less agreeable to God, when accompanied with many distractions; on the contrary, it may be more useful than if we had many consolations, because it is more laborious: provided, however, that we have the wish to withdraw from those distractions, and do not allow our mind to dwell on them willingly.

The very same observation applies to the difficulty which, during the day, we feel to fix our mind on God, and on heavenly things: provided we endeavor to keep our thoughts from running after trifles, and learn patience, by not growing weary of our labor, which is suffered for the love of God.

We must distinguish between God and a perception of God, between faith and a feeling of faith. A person about to suffer martyrdom for God does not always think of God at that time; and though he has no feeling of faith, yet he does not cease to merit, or to perform an act of the greatest love. It is the same with the presence of God. We must content ourselves with considering that He is our God, and we are His weak creatures, unworthy of that honor; thus St. Francis spent a whole night, saying to God, "Who art Thou, O Lord, and who am I?"

He who, in praying to God, perceives that he prays, is not perfectly attentive to prayer; for he turns away his attention from God to think on the prayer which he offers. Even the care that we have not to have distractions, is often a very great distraction: simplicity in spiritual actions is their most commendable quality. Would you wish to behold God? Behold Him then, and be attentive to that; for if you begin to reflect and to examine how you look yourself while you are looking on Him, it is no longer God you are viewing, but yourself. He who is occupied in fervent prayer pays no attention as to whether he is engaged in prayer or not, for he thinks not of the prayer which he makes, but of God to whom he makes it. He who burns with the ardor of sacred love, does not recall his heart to consider what it does, but keeps it fixed on God, employed in loving Him, with whose love it is consumed. The heavenly chorister takes so much pleasure in pleasing his God, that he finds no pleasure in the melody of his voice, unless because it pleases his God.

Chapter Twelve

Consolation in Temptation

B E NOT troubled, however great the temptations that assail you. Let the enemy rage at the door; let him stamp, thump, romp, yell; do the worst in his power; we are sure he cannot enter but by the door of our consent. Let us keep it closed, often taking a look to see that it is properly fastened, and there is nothing to fear.

Humble yourself very much, and be not at all surprised. The lilies that grow among thorns are the whitest. *What does he know who has not been tempted?*

It is a misfortune that you dread temptations so much. Be assured that all the temptations of Hell cannot sully a soul which is displeased with them; let them do their worst then. The Apostle St. Paul suffered terrible ones, and God, out of love for him, would not remove them. Come, come, have courage; let this heart belong to Jesus, and let the mastiff bark at the door as long as he pleases. Join the sweet

Jesus and His sweet Mother in the midst of darkness, nails, thorns, lances, derelictions.[1] Live for a time in tears, without obtaining anything; God will at length rejoice you, and grant you the desire of your heart. But even if He should not, let us not cease to serve Him, for He does not cease to be our God, and the affection that we owe to Him should be immortal and imperishable.

I observe very distinctly the ant hill of inclinations that self-love nourishes and spreads over your heart, and I know quite well that the nature of your subtile, delicate, and fertile mind, contributes something thereto; but still, they are only inclinations, and since you are annoyed by their importunity, there is no reason to suppose that they are accepted by any consent, or at least by any deliberate consent.

No, your dear soul, having conceived the great desire with which God has inspired it to belong to Him, could not easily consent to any contrary design. Your heart may be shaken by its passions; but I think it can rarely sin by consent. "Miserable man that I am," said the great Apostle, "Who will deliver me from this body of death?"

He perceives a regular army, composed of his humors and aversions, natural habits and earthly inclinations, that have determined on his spiritual death; and because he fears them, he testifies that he hates them; and because he hates

---

1 "What I have said suffices to show with how much contempt every true Christian should regard those phantoms by which the devils endeavor to terrify him. Let him know that as often as a soul despises its adversaries, it weakens them, and acquires sway over them; each new attack brings it some new advantage. I clearly see their impotence; faithful to God, no one need be afraid. They are strong only against those careless souls who capitulate without a battle, and who receive on surrender that treatment which is administered by despots."—*St. Teresa of Avila.*

them, he cannot endure them without grief; and his grief finds expression in this affecting exclamation, to which he replies himself by saying that *the grace of God through Jesus Christ should preserve him,* not from fear, or from terror, or from alarm, or from battle, but from defeat.

"It is true," you say; "but I have already often taken the knife to cut off and circumcise my passions; I have done all, as appears to me, that I possibly could, employing much time, with very great care and vigilance, yet I still experience the same aversions, disgusts, and repugnances." Ah! My dear soul, do you not know that we are not in this world for enjoyment, but for suffering? Wait awhile, until you are in Heaven, and then you will possess a full peace and a perfect contentment—exempt from all the irregular motions of a nature vitiated and corrupted by sin—a tranquility and repose unalterable, because it is there we are to enjoy peace, and not in this life, where we must suffer, and must circumcise ourselves. He who would live here without passions would not suffer, but enjoy himself, which cannot be; for as long as we live, we shall have passions, and shall never be free from them before death, according to the opinion of doctors, received by the Church. But why be in trouble, since in combating those passions and motions lies our victory, our triumph, our glory?[2]

To be in this world, and not to feel any emotion of

---

2 "*Blessed,*" says St. James, "*is he who suffers temptation; for when he shall have borne this trial, he shall receive the crown of life,* and enjoy, not only in Heaven, but while still living on earth, a perfect beatitude in the depth of his heart, united to our king, Jesus, by a pure and holy love. Hope not to enter into an intimate union with the God of sanctity, without first being sanctified by the cross. *Be ye holy,* says God, *for I am holy.*"—*Olier.*

passion, is an inconsistency. The glorious St. Bernard says that it is heresy to assert that we can persevere in one same state here below, inasmuch as the Holy Ghost, speaking by the mouth of Job, concerning man, declares that *he never remains in the same state.* This is an answer to your complaints regarding the levity and inconstancy of your soul; for I believe, without a doubt, that it is continually beaten about by the winds of its passions, and consequently is always in commotion; but I believe as firmly that the grace of God and your good resolutions remain steady in the summit of your soul, where the standard of the cross is firmly planted, and where faith, hope, and charity exclaim aloud: "Live Jesus!"

Take notice of this: so long as the temptation displeases you, there is nothing to fear; for why does it displease you, but because you do not approve of it? These importunate temptations come from the malice of the devil; but the pain we feel on their account comes from the mercy of God, who, in opposition to the will and from the wickedness of our enemy, draws a holy tribulation by which He refines the gold intended for His treasury.[3]

I say, then, that your temptations are from the devil and Hell, but your afflictions are from God and Heaven; the mothers are from Babylon, but the daughters are from Jerusalem. Despise the vain allurement; embrace the precious tribulation.

It is necessary for the soldier to be victorious in war, to

---

3 "To unite oneself to God without directly combating a temptation is a very efficacious mode of not yielding to it. By this means we find in Jesus Christ what we cannot find in ourselves."—*Bossuet.*

be at his ease in peace. Never shall we possess perfect meekness and charity, unless we are exercised in repugnances, aversions, and disgusts. True peace does not consist in never fighting, but is found after victory. The vanquished no longer combat, yet they do not enjoy true peace. We should be exceedingly humbled to see that we are yet so little masters of ourselves, and so much attached to our own ease and repose.

We shall obtain no recompense without victory, no victory without war. Have courage, then, and by converting your pain, which is without remedy, into merit, make a virtue of necessity. Look often to Our Lord, who regards you, poor little creature as you are, amid your labors and distractions. He will send you aid, and will bless your afflictions. You should, on this consideration, take patiently and quietly the tediousness that grieves you, and bear it meekly for the love of Him who only permits it for your good.

Elevate, then, your heart frequently to God, beg His assistance, and let your chief consolation be the happiness of belonging to Him. Every object of displeasure will be of little account when you remember that you have so kind a friend, so great a support, so excellent a refuge.

CHAPTER THIRTEEN

DIFFIDENCE AND CONFIDENCE

D IFFIDENCE in our own strength does not mean a want of resolution, but is a true acknowledgment of our misery. It is far better to diffide in our power of resisting temptations, than to imagine ourselves sufficiently strong and secure, provided that what we cannot expect from our own strength, we do expect from the grace of God.

Many who, in the midst of great consolation, promised to do wonders for God, have, on coming to the point, failed completely; and many who were possessed of a great distrust of their own strength, and a great fear that they should fail on a trying occasion, have, at the moment, done wonders: because this sense of their weakness impelled them to seek help from God, to watch, to pray, and to be humble, so as not to enter into temptation.

I say that though we should not feel within us any strength or courage to resist temptation, were it immediately presented to us, yet, provided we desire to resist it, and hope that, if it came, God would assist us, and we should ask His aid, there is no reason for us to be sad, inasmuch as it is not necessary always to feel strength and courage, but it is sufficient that we hope to have them at the proper time and place; and there is no need that we should perceive in ourselves any sign or mark that we shall have them, but it suffices that we hope to receive succor from God.

Samson, the strongest of men, did not perceive the supernatural strength with which God had invested him, unless on rare occasions; and hence it is said that when he met with lions or enemies, the Spirit of God seized upon him to destroy them. Thus God, who does nothing in vain, gives us strength and courage only when we require them; and, therefore, we must always hope that in every occurrence, He will aid us, if we invoke Him. We should often employ these words of David: "Why art thou sorrowful, O my soul? And why dost thou trouble me? Hope in the Lord;" and that prayer he used: "When my strength forsakes me, O Lord! Thou wilt not abandon me." Very well, now, since you desire to belong entirely to God, why do you fear your weakness, though I do not mean you to place any reliance on it? Do you hope in God? And shall he who hopes in God ever be confounded? No, never. I conjure you, then, to silence those vain sophisms that arise in your mind; no other answer is necessary than that you desire to be faithful on all occasions, and hope, without testing your soul as to its future dispositions, that in every time God will enable you to serve Him faithfully. Many who are brave in the absence of an enemy, show little valor in his presence; and, on the other hand, many who tremble before the battle, are the boldest in the hour of danger: we should not be afraid of fear.

Walk always near to God, for the gentleness of His shadow is more salutary than the brightness of the sun.

It is not wrong to tremble sometimes before Him in whose presence the angels themselves tremble, when they behold His majesty: but on condition that holy love, which predominates over all His works, should hold the highest place in our souls, as it should be the beginning and the end of all our considerations.

Chapter Fourteen

Remedy for Temptations against Purity

R EMAIN in peace in the midst of temptations: faith, hope, and charity, well fixed in our hearts, are not likely to be shaken, though exposed to the breeze: how can we expect our resolutions to be undisturbed? You are certainly deserving of admiration if you cannot be content with having your trees deeply and firmly planted, but also desire that not a leaf should be stirred.

No, no, let the wind blow; and mistake not the rustling of the leaves for the crash of arms. I was lately near a bee hive, and some of the bees flew out on my face. I put up my hand to drive them away. "Stop," said a countryman, "there is no fear, do not touch them, and they will not hurt you; if you touch them, they will sting you." I believed his word, and not one of them injured me.

Now, if you believe my word, do not fear those

temptations, or touch them, and they will not do you the least harm. Pass by, and give yourself no concern.

We may use a variety of plans on such occasions. Sometimes it is well to make a few acts of the love of God, and of confidence in His grace; then not to fear being carried away by those little attacks against our resolutions. They are groundless annoyances; for, if the angel of darkness, buffeting St. Paul by so many agitations, could not make him offend against purity, why should we imagine that our resolutions are broken on similar occasions?

Answer not a word to the shameful thoughts that come upon you; only say to Our Lord from your heart: O my God! Thou knowest that I honor Thee; I am all Thine. *Dispute not* with the temptation.

Here, alas! Is a good soul greatly tempted. Let it be exceedingly humbled, but not astonished: the lilies that grow among thorns are the whitest. *What does he know, who has not been tempted?* It may change the bodily exercise, if the pain lie in the thoughts; if it cannot conveniently change the occupation, let it change the posture; by this diversity, it will find relief. If the pain fill the imagination, it is good to sing, to join the company of others, or to pass from one spiritual exercise to another. Above all, let the soul not be astonished, but frequently renew its vows, and be humbled before God. Let it promise itself victory through the intercession of the Blessed Virgin.

If anything remain as a scruple, let it mention the matter boldly and courageously, on going to Confession. But I trust in God that with a noble mind it will keep free from everything that could be a cause of scruple. I would wish it to use the hairshirt once a week, unless it finds that, by doing so, it becomes more sluggish in the performance of more important exercises, as sometimes happens.

Chapter Fifteen

Mode of Combating Temptations against Faith

YOUR temptations against faith have returned, and though you do not reply to them by a single syllable, yet they press hard upon you.

You do not reply to them; so far, good; but you think upon them, you are alarmed at them, you tremble for them; only for this, they would not do you any hurt. You are too sensitive about temptations. You love your faith, and would not wish to have one thought contrary to it; hence, immediately when a thought touches your mind, you are saddened and troubled. You are too jealous of the purity of faith; everything appears to you capable of tainting it.

We must act in this temptation as in that against chastity: neither dispute with it much or little; but do as the children of Israel did with the bones of the Paschal lamb, which they would not attempt to break, but cast whole into the fire. We must not answer or appear to understand what the enemy says. Let him brawl as long as he pleases at the door; we need only say: Who's there?

That is true, you will tell me; but he annoys me, and the noise he makes outside is so great that I cannot understand or arrange anything well within. Patience! We shall speak by signs, we shall prostrate ourselves before the Lord, and remain at His feet; He will understand by this humble behavior that you are His, and that you desire His assistance, while unable to ask it. But especially take care not to open the door within, either to see who is without, or to chase the vagabond; at length he will cease his noise, and leave you in peace.

It will soon be time, you tell me. Courage! Then; it will soon be time; provided that he does not enter, all is right. It is a very good sign if our enemy knocks and storms at the door, for it shows that he is not where he would wish to be. If it were open, he would no longer cry out, he would enter, and take a seat. Remember this, so as not to fall into scrupulosity.

I desire that we should be simple and settled in that faith which the holy Church teaches us, believing firmly everything that is written on this rock: for the evangelical law is written on it. Let us believe firmly, and submit our understanding to that Church which Our Lord built upon the rock; for the gates of Hell shall never prevail against it. Our Lord prayed for St. Peter that his faith might not fail: this is the head of that Church which is the pillar and the ground of truth, as St. Paul says to his dear Timothy. "Blessed is he who dashes his little ones against

the rock," says the Psalmist. When you are surprised sometimes with strange fancies concerning the things of faith,
with little imaginations and thoughts of infidelity, what
will you do? If you allow them to enter into your mind
they will trouble you, and take away your peace; break and
shatter those thoughts and imaginations to pieces against
the rock of the Church, and say to your understanding:
Ah! My understanding, God has not commanded thee
to feed thyself; it is for Peter and his successors to feed
thee; blessed then is he who breaks his little ones against
this rock.

I shall now give you another remedy. Temptations
against faith go directly to the understanding to lead it to
disputations, to reveries, to dreams. Do you know how
you should act while the enemy amuses himself about the
means of scaling your intellect? Start out presently by the
door of your will, and give him a good shot; that is to say, as
soon as the temptation against faith makes its appearance,
attack it. But how do this? And how do that? And what if
this happens? And what if that happens? Instead of entering
into any discourse or discussion with the enemy, let your
effective force with all its strength rush upon him, and, at
the same time, joining the exterior to the interior voice,
cry out: Ah! Wretched traitor! You forsook the Church of
the Angels, and would you wish me to forsake that of the
Saints? Disloyal, unfaithful, and perfidious, you presented
the first woman with the apple of perdition, and would
you wish me to taste it too? *Begone, Satan! For it is written:
thou shalt not tempt the Lord thy God;* no, I will not argue
or contend with you: Eve, wishing to do so, was seduced;

Eve, yielding, was lost; live Jesus, in whom I believe! Live the Church, to which I adhere!

We must also say to Jesus Christ and to the Holy Spirit such other things as they will suggest, and to the Church: O mother of the children of God! Never shall I be separated from thee! I wish to live and die within thy pale!

I do not know whether I have made myself well understood. I mean to say that we should retaliate with affections and not with reasons, with virtues and not with considerations. It is true that during the time of temptation, the poor will is as dry as a stick; but so much the better; its blows will be the more terrible on the enemy, who, when he sees that instead of retarding your progress, he only gives you occasion to exercise a thousand virtuous affections, and particularly to make protestations of faith, will very soon leave you altogether.

To conclude: these temptations, like others, are but afflictions; and we must rely upon the assurance of Holy Scripture: "Blessed is he who endures temptation; for having been proved, he shall receive the crown of life." I must inform you that I have seen few persons advanced in holiness without this trial, and therefore we must have patience. Our God will send the calm after the storm.

CHAPTER SIXTEEN

TEMPTATIONS OF BLASPHEMY AND INFIDELITY

YOU cannot and you should not believe that tempta-tions of blasphemy and infidelity[1] come from God; and whoever taught you that God was their author? It were all right, if you spoke of darkness; all right, of derelic-tion and deprivation of strength; all right, of diarrhea in the spiritual stomach; all right, of bitterness in the interior mouth, which makes the sweetest wine of this world bit-ter; but of suggestions of blasphemy and infidelity, ah! No. They cannot come from our good God; His bosom is too pure for such conceptions.

Do you know how God acts in this case? He permits the wicked blacksmith who turns out such articles of work-manship to come and offer them to us for sale, in order that

---

[1] Temptations of infidelity—that is, temptations against the virtue of faith. —*Publisher*, 2013.

by our contempt for those miserable wares we may testify our affection for divine things. Thus He acted with Job, with St. Anthony, with St. Catherine of Siena, with many good souls whom I have known, and with my own soul, which is worthless, and which I have not known.

Well, then, is there any need to be vexed? Let him cool himself, and do you keep every avenue barricaded; he will depart at length, or, if not, God will compel him to raise the siege. Remember what I think I told you before; it is a very good sign that he makes so much noise and disturbance outside the will, for it shows he is not inside. And courage! So long as we can say with resolution, though without consolation: Live Jesus! There is nothing to fear.

Do not tell me that you seem to say it like a coward, without strength or courage, and only by doing violence to yourself. O God! This is that holy violence which bears away the kingdom of Heaven.

Your apprehensions may show that the outworks have been taken, that the enemy has captured the entire fortress, but still the citadel remains impregnable, and can only fall with its defender.

This defender is our free will, which, naked before God, resides in the highest and most spiritual portion of the soul, without any other support than God and itself; when every other faculty of the soul is disturbed by the enemy, it alone remains perfect master of itself to yield or not to yield.

But, you see, souls are afflicted, because the enemy, holding possession of all the other faculties, raises in them a frightful tumult and uproar. Scarcely can we understand what is said, scarcely can the superior will make one movement. Its voice is clearer, softer, finer than that of the inferior will, but the harsh, rough tones of the latter drown the former.[2]

---

2   The following beautiful thoughts are from the Blessed Henry Suso, O.P.; they are well calculated to comfort souls subject to those horrible temptations: "I shall add, to terminate this subject, that the temptations of blasphemy, despair, and interior shame, place to a certain degree those who resist them in the rank and prerogatives of martyrs; for the servants of God would much prefer to yield with one blow their heads, their blood, their life, for Jesus Christ, than to endure such painful temptations for months, and even for years. Let us conclude then that persons afflicted with scruples are the most favored by divine love, and the surest to arrive at Heaven, because by enduring their pains with patience and humility, and thus dying to themselves, they live in a continual Purgatory, and leave this earth only to fly to Heaven, purified from every matter of expiation. This is what happened to a holy soul that was cruelly tried by the temptations of which we have spoken. God glorified it at the moment of death, conducted it to Heaven without requiring it to pass through the flames of Purgatory, and of its salvation I can render testimony, to the praise and honor of Jesus Christ, who is blessed forever."

CHAPTER SEVENTEEN

MANNER OF BEHAVING IN THE TEMPTATIONS OF SELF-LOVE

LOVE of ourselves, esteem of ourselves, false freedom of spirit, are roots which cannot be easily plucked out of the human heart; but we can prevent their bearing any fruits, which are sins; as for their starts or buddings, we cannot prevent them altogether, so long as we are in this life, though we can moderate their dimensions by the practice of contrary virtues, especially by the love of God.

We must then have patience, and little by little retrench our evil habits, overcome our inclinations, and subdue our aversions; for, in a word, my dearest daughter, this life is a continual warfare, and who is he that can say: I am not attacked?

Repose is reserved for Heaven, where the palm of victory awaits us. On earth we must always struggle between fear and hope, with the condition that hope shall ever be the stronger, in consideration of the omnipotence of Him who helps us.

Self-love never dies but when we die; it has a thousand means of concealment in our soul, so that we cannot dislodge it. It is the eldest born of the soul, it is natural to us. It heads a battalion of rifles, with dreadful mutinies, stratagems, passions. Nothing can be more adroit; it has a thousand quick evolutions.

We must always expect either its open attacks or its secret influences so long as we are in this land of exile; it suffices that we do not yield to it with a full, steady, deliberate consent. The virtue of holy indifference is so excellent that our old man, or human nature, according to its natural faculties, was not capable of it; not even in Our Lord, who, as a child of Adam, though exempt from sin and all its appurtenances, was not, according to His natural faculties, indifferent to events, but desired not to die on the cross: perfect indifference being reserved to the supreme portion of the soul, to the faculties glowing with grace, to the "new man."

Little surprises of passion are unavoidable in this mortal life, on which account the great Apostle cries to Heaven: *Alas! Poor wretch that I am!* I feel two different men within me, the old and the new; two laws, the law of the senses, and the law of the spirit; two operations, that of nature and that of grace. *Who will deliver me from the body of this death?*

This is the reason why we have not that consolation we ought to have when we see good done; for what we do not see in ourselves is not so sweet or agreeable to us as what we see there, because we love ourselves too tenderly and delicately.

Self-love makes us desire to do such and such a thing of our own choice, but we would not desire to do it if of another's choice, or from obedience.

On the other hand, if we possessed the perfection of the love of God, we would far prefer to do what is commanded, because it proceeds more from the love of God, and less from ourselves.

Your way is very good, and there is nothing to be said against it, unless that, considering the length of your steps, you go rather fast and run the risk of falling. You make too many reflections on those sallies of your self-love, which are indeed frequent, but not dangerous, so long as without being wearied at their importunity or astonished at their multiplicity, you quietly say one little "No." Walk in simplicity; desire not so much repose of mind, and you shall find more.

Why do you put yourself in pain? God is good, He knows well what you are; your inclinations cannot injure you, bad as they are, since they are left in you only to exercise your superior will in effecting a more advantageous union with the will of God. Keep your eyes raised on high, my dearest daughter, by a perfect confidence in the goodness of God. Be not too busy about Him, for He told Martha that He did not wish it. He would prefer us not to be so anxious, even to do good.

Do not examine your soul and its progress so closely. You should not wish to be so perfect, but with good faith pass your life in those exercises and employments which await you from time to time. Be not solicitous for the morrow. God, who has guided you until the present day, will guide you to the end. Rely peacefully, with a holy and loving confidence, on the sweet arrangements of Divine Providence.

It is folly to be astonished at finding self-love within us; for it never leaves us. It sleeps sometimes like a fox; then suddenly awakes; we must therefore with constancy watch it, and with patience defend ourselves. If it sometimes wounds us, we are healed by retracting what it has made us say, and disowning what it has made us do. The sallies of self-love should be neglected. By disowning them two or three times a day, we are set free. It is not necessary to drive them out by the neck, it suffices to say one little "No."

Let us then remain in peace. When we happen to offend against the laws of indifference in things indifferent, carried away by some sudden fit of self-love or of the passions, let us as soon as possible lay our heart before God, let us say to Him in a spirit of confidence and humility: "Mercy! Lord! For I am weak." Let us then arise in peace and tranquility, and renew the thread of our indifference, to continue our work.

There is no need to tear the chords or to throw away the lute because we have perceived a little discord; we must listen to find out whence the discord arises, and tighten or slacken the strings as the art requires.

The inclinations of pride, of vanity, of self-love, are blended with our life, and whether sensibly or insensibly, introduce their sentiments into almost all our actions; but still they are not the motives of our actions. St. Bernard one day feeling that they attacked him while he preached, said:

"Depart from me, Satan! It was not for you I began, and it is not for you I will finish."

One single thing I have to say to you regarding what you wrote to me, that you nourish pride by affectation in your discourse and in your correspondence. In language, indeed, affectation sometimes glides in so insensibly that we do not perceive it; but if we chance to take notice of it, we should immediately change the style. In letters it is much more insupportable, for we better see what we are doing, and if we find any notable affectation, we must punish the hand that wrote it, by obliging it to write another letter after some other fashion.

I doubt not but that amid so many turns and windings of the heart, a few venial faults may creep in, but as they are not serious, they will not deprive us of the fruit of our resolutions; they will only keep away the pleasure that would arise from steering clear of all failure, if the state of this life permitted such a thing.

Moreover, be just; neither accuse nor excuse your poor soul until after mature consideration, for fear that if you excuse it without reason, you may render it insolent, and if you accuse it without grounds, you may render it pusillanimous. Walk with simplicity, and you will walk with confidence.

That multitude of thoughts bustling about your mind should on no account be attacked, for when would you succeed in destroying them one after another? It is only necessary from time to time, I mean many times a day, to deny them entrance altogether, to shut them out in a body, and then to let them play as many freaks at the door of your heart as they choose: provided they do not enter, it is little matter. Remain in peace, and be not troubled, for God is on your side.

Chapter Eighteen

The Just Man Falls and Rises without Perceiving It

IT IS not said in that passage of Scripture which is so frequently quoted, that the just man sees or perceives himself falling seven times a day, but that he falls seven times a day; so he rises often without perceiving that he rises. Wherefore, you are not to be in pain; yet you can mention, if you choose, anything you may have remarked; committing it to the sweet mercy of Him who places His hand under those who fall without malice, that they may not be hurt, and raises them again so quickly and so gently, that they neither perceive they have fallen, because He received them, nor that they are lifted up, because He assisted them so suddenly that they have not time to think of it.

Do as little children do: while they see their mother holding them by the sleeve, they walk courageously, run about everywhere, and are not the least surprised at the trips and stoppages they sometimes meet with, through the weakness of their limbs. Thus while you perceive God holding you by the good will and resolution He has given you to serve Him, walk courageously, and be not astonished at the jolts you get now and again. There is no cause to be grumbling about them, but at intervals cast yourself into His arms and give Him the kiss of charity. Go joyfully, with an open heart; if you cannot always go as joyfully as you would wish, at least go always confidently. Our Lord acts towards us just in the same manner as a good mother, who allows her child to walk alone on a soft meadow, where the grass is thick, or on a mossy bank, because she knows that if it falls, it will not be hurt, but on the rough, dangerous road she carries it carefully in her arms. We have often seen souls, who endured manfully the greatest assaults without being overcome, yet fell a little after before a mere shadow. And why was it so, unless because Our Lord knowing that they would not be much the worse of it, allowed them to walk alone in an easy place, which He would not do along the perilous precipices of great temptations, where the hand of His omnipotence would be indispensably necessary?

Chapter Nineteen

A Good Sadness and a Bad Sadness

SADNESS may be either good or bad.

"The sadness which is according to God," says St. Paul, "Worketh penance unto salvation, and the sadness of the world worketh death." Sadness can then be good or bad, according to the different effects it produces in us. In truth it has more bad than good effects, for it has only two of the latter, namely, mercy and penance, while it has six of the former, namely, anguish, idleness, indignation, jealousy, envy, and impatience. This made the Wise Man say that *sadness has killed many,* and that *there is nothing to be gained by it,* because for the two good little streams that flow from it, there are six very bad ones.

The enemy makes use of sadness to try the perseverance of the good: for, as he endeavors to rejoice the wicked in their sins, so he endeavors to sadden the just in their good works, and as he cannot draw them to evil unless by making them find it pleasant, so he cannot turn them away from good unless by making them find it wearisome. The devil asks only for sadness and melancholy; and as he is sad and melancholy himself, and will be so eternally, he wishes that everyone else should become like him.

Bad sadness troubles the soul, throws it into uneasiness, inspires it with inordinate fears, and fills it with disgust for prayer; stupefies and confuses the brain; deprives the soul of counsel, resolution, judgment, courage, and entirely abases its powers. In a word, it is like a severe winter, which banishes all beauty from the earth, and benumbs the very animals; or it robs the soul of all consolation, and strikes its every faculty with helplessness.[1]

King David does not complain of sadness alone, saying, "Why art thou sad, O my soul?" but chiefly of trouble and uneasiness, adding: "Why dost thou trouble me?" A good sadness leaves great peace and tranquility in the soul. On this account, Our Lord, after having said to His Apostles: "You shall be sad," adds: "Let not your heart be troubled, nor let it be afraid." "In peace is my bitterness most bitter," says Isaias. Bad sadness comes like a hailstorm, with an unexpected change, and great impetuosity, and so suddenly that we cannot tell whence it comes; for it has no foundation. But after its arrival, it seeks on all sides to be

---

1   "Bad sadness casts down the soul, makes it lose confidence in God and relish for holy exercises, and encourages it to seek amusements without, to distract it from that which it suffers within; the other, on the contrary, if you really wish to give the name of sadness to that sorrow so worthy of a Christian, inclines one to prayer and fervor in the service of God, spreads a divine unction through the soul, and moves it to seek solitude and intercourse with God, in whom alone it finds its consolation."
—P. Lombez.

obeyed; while good sadness comes sweetly into the soul like a gentle rain, and with rational antecedents.

Bad sadness ruins the heart, dulling and deadening it, and making it abandon the care of the work, as the Psalmist says, or as Agar did when she left her son under the tree to go and weep. Good sadness gives strength and courage, and does not allow us to leave off or abandon a good design: such was the sadness of Our Lord, which, although so great that there never was the like, yet it did not prevent Him from praying and having care of His disciples. And Our Lady, having lost her Son, was most sad; yet it did not hinder her from seeking Him diligently—as did Magdalen also—without waiting to lament and weep in vain.

Bad sadness darkens the understanding, takes away counsel, resolution, and judgment from the soul, as happened to those of whom the Psalmist says: "They were troubled and reeled like a drunken man; and all their wisdom was swallowed up." (*Psalm* 106:27). We seek for remedies here and there confusedly, without knowing what we do, and as it were groping our way. Good sadness opens the mind, makes it serene and luminous, and as the Psalmist says, gives understanding.

Bad sadness gives a disgust for prayer and a distrust of the goodness of God; good sadness, on the contrary, proceeding from God, increases our confidence in Him, and makes us pray and invoke His mercy. *Tribulation and anguish have troubled me; but Thy commandments have been my meditation.*

In short, those who are possessed of a bad sadness have

their souls troubled with ever so many horrors, errors, and useless fears, with dread of being abandoned by God, of being in His disfavor, of being unfit to appear before Him in order to ask pardon. Everything seems to go contrary to their salvation; they are like Cain, who thought everyone he should meet would kill him. They think that God is unjust towards them, and will be severe to them even to eternity, and that it is all in their regard alone, while the rest of the world is perfectly happy at their expense: all which proceeds from a secret pride, persuading them that they ought to be better and more fervent than others, more perfect than anyone else.[2]

But good sadness discourses in this manner: "I am a miserable, vile, and abject creature, and therefore God will show me mercy; for power is made perfect in infirmity, and there is nothing astonishing in being poor and miserable."

Now, the foundation of the difference that exists between good and bad sadness is that the Holy Spirit is the author of good sadness, and, because He is the true Comforter, His operations are ever accompanied with sweetness and light.

In fine, since He is the true good, His operations cannot be separated from the true good; and "The fruits of

---

2 Reflect that sadness is good for nothing; that far from remedying the smallest evil, it is in itself a great evil; that it destroys our health, shortens our life, prevents us from enjoying piety and advancing in virtue, and puts our eternal salvation in danger; it makes us disagreeable to God and man, and insupportable to ourselves; no person likes to see us sad except our enemies, and particularly the enemies of our salvation; we become, in this state, the scourge of society, the shame of our neighbors, the affliction of our friends, the mocking stock of our enemies, the outcast of all. If we retire into solitude, we are worn out with *ennui,* and if we give ourselves to the affairs of public life, we succeed as ill; we are good for nothing. Everything tires us, everything is insupportable to us; time lasts too long for us, and life itself is a burden to us.

the Holy Ghost," says St. Paul, "Are charity, joy, peace, patience, benignity, longanimity."

On the contrary, the wicked spirit, who is the author of a bad sadness—for I do not here speak of natural sadness, which has more need of physicians than of theologians—is truly a gloomy and perplexing destroyer, and its fruits can only be hatred, melancholy, uneasiness, chagrin, languor, malice. Lastly, all the marks of a bad sadness are also the marks of a bad timidity.

CHAPTER TWENTY

HOW CONTRARY SADNESS IS TO DIVINE LOVE

WE CANNOT engraft an oak on a pear tree, so contrary are these two trees to each other. We can no more engraft anger or despair on charity. As for despair, unless we reduce it to a just diffidence of ourselves, or rather to that reasonable sentiment we ought to have of the vanity, weakness, and inconstancy of the favors, helps, and promises of the world, I do not know what service divine love can draw from it.[1]

How can sadness be useful to holy charity, since among the fruits of the Holy Ghost, joy holds the very next

---

1 "Have pity on your soul by making it agreeable to God, repress all your evil desires, center the sentiments of your heart in the sanctity of God, and drive sadness from you; for it has killed many, and is of no advantage." This is the counsel of the Wise Man, or rather of the Holy Spirit.

Be not discouraged; miseries, frailties, etc., are diseases, but discouragement is a kind of death.

Sadness serves only to increase the pains of this life.

place to charity? Nevertheless the great Apostle speaks thus: "The sadness which is according to God worketh penance unto salvation, but the sadness of the world worketh death. There is then a sadness according to God;" which is exercised either by sinners in penance, or by the good in compassion for the temporal miseries of the neighbor, or by the perfect in deploring the spiritual calamities of souls; for David, St. Peter, Magdalen, wept over their sins; Agar wept seeing her son nearly dead of thirst, Jeremias wept over the ruin of Jerusalem, Our Lord over the Jews, and His great Apostle mourning uttered these words: "Many walk, of whom I have often told you and now tell you again, weeping, that they are enemies of the cross of Jesus Christ."

There is, also, a *sadness of this world,* which proceeds from three causes:

1. It sometimes proceeds from the infernal enemy, who, by a thousand sad, melancholy, and vexatious suggestions, darkens the understanding, weakens the will, and troubles the whole soul; and, as a thick fog fills the head and chest with cold, by this means rendering respiration difficult and throwing the traveler into perplexity, so the devil, filling the human mind with sad thoughts, takes away its facility of making aspirations to God, and thus casts it into an extreme weariness and discouragement. It is said that there is a fish called the devil of the sea, which, heaving up the mud, discolors the water all around it, in order to conceal itself, as in an ambush, from which, when it perceives the poor little fishes, it suddenly rushes out, tearing and devouring them: whence, perhaps, comes the expression of "fishing in troubled waters," which we hear so frequently

used. Now, it is just the same with the devil of Hell as with the devil of the sea; for he lays his ambush in sadness, and, having troubled the soul with a multitude of distressing thoughts, cast here and there through the understanding, he rushes out afterwards on the affections, crushing them down with doubts, jealousies, aversions, envies, apprehensions, and supplying a variety of vain, bitter, and melancholy subtleties, in order that we may reject all kinds of reasons and consolations in our wants.

2. Sadness proceeds at other times from our natural condition, when the melancholic humor predominates within us, and though this is evidently not vicious in itself, yet the enemy makes great use of it to brew a thousand temptations in our souls; for, as spiders only make their webs when the weather is dark and the sky cloudy, so the devil has never the same ease in laying the snares of his suggestions around sweet, benign, and gay souls, as he has when in the presence of melancholy, gloomy, and hypochondriac ones; for he easily agitates the latter with chagrins, murmurs, hatreds, envies, and a thousand dark suspicions.

3. There is a sadness which the variety of human occurrences brings upon us. "What joy can I have," said Tobias, "Not being able to see the light of heaven?" Thus Jacob was sad at the news of the death of his Joseph, and David at that of his Absalom. Now, this sadness is common to the good and to the bad, but with the good it is moderated by acquiescence in and resignation to the will of God, as we see in Tobias, who, for all the adversities that befell him, returned thanks to the Divine Majesty, and in Job, who

blessed the name of the Lord for afflictions, and in Daniel, who changed his sorrows into canticles. On the contrary, with worldlings, this sadness is an ordinary companion and changes only into regrets, despair, and giddiness of mind; for they are like monkeys and marmots, which are always peevish, cross, and troublesome at the waning of the moon, as at its increase they jump, dance and play their pranks to no end. The worldling is surly, sullen, and snappish in the absence of prosperity; and in its full flow, he is invariably a conceited and insolent blusterer.

Indeed, the sadness of true penance does not so much deserve the name of sadness as of displeasure against sin, or detestation of sin: a sadness which is never vexed or morose; a sadness which does not enervate the mind, but makes it active, prompt, and diligent; a sadness which dispirits not the heart, but elevates it to prayer and hope, and excites the fervor of devotion; a sadness which always, even in the height of its bitterness, produces the sweetness of an incomparable consolation, according to the words of the great St. Augustine: "Let the penitent be always sad, but let him always rejoice in his sadness." "The sadness," says Cassian, "which works a solid penance and an agreeable repentance, of which we never repent, is obedient, affable, humble, kind, gracious, patient, as being the offspring of charity: so much so, that, reaching to every pain of body and mind, it is in a manner joyful, reanimated, and re-invigorated, by the prospect of its advantage; it retains all the sweetness of benignity and longanimity, having with it the fruits of the Holy Ghost mentioned by the Apostle: "Now, the fruits of the Holy Ghost are charity, joy, peace, longanimity,

goodness, benignity, faith, meekness, continence." Such is
true penance, and such is a good sadness, which, properly
speaking, is not at all sad or melancholy, but only attentive
and resolute to detest and reject sin, both past and future,
for the sole love of God, whom sin displeases, that is to
say, without the admixture of any imperfect love, without
interested views of promised reward or punishment.

This loving repentance is usually practiced by frequent
aspirations or elevations of the heart to God, after the
example of the ancient penitents. Thus:

> I am thine, O my God, save me, have mercy
> on me, for my soul has trusted in Thee; save
> me, O Lord, for the waters overwhelm my
> heart; make me as one of Thy hired ser-
> vants; O Lord! Be propitious to me: to me
> a poor sinner.

In this sense, we say that prayer justifies; for penitent
prayer, or suppliant repentance, elevates the soul to God,
and, uniting it to His goodness, undoubtedly obtains pardon in virtue of the love which animates it.

Many a time we see a repentance, eager, troubled,
impatient, weeping, bitter, sighing, uneasy, sour, and melancholy, which in the end is found unfruitful, and without
any true amendment, because it does not proceed from the
true motives of the virtue of penance, but from self-love
and natural love.

The sadness of the world worketh death, says the Apostle.
We must then carefully avoid it, and banish it according to
our power. If it be natural, we should drive it off by diverting

its movements in suitable exercises, and by attending to the remedies and mode of life which physicians judge proper. If it proceed from temptations, we should discover our heart to our spiritual father, who will prescribe us the means of overcoming them, according to that which we have said in the Fourth Part of the *Introduction to a Devout Life*. If it be accidental, we should have recourse to that which is laid down in the Eighth Book, in order to see how amiable tribulations are to the children of God, and how the greatness of our hopes in eternal life should render almost unworthy of a thought the trifling and transitory occurrences of this life.

There are some actions that depend on physical power; hence, however melancholy one may be, he can still, though without much pleasure, say kind and civil words, and notwithstanding his inclinations, perform from reason things conformable in word and work to charity and courtesy. A person is excusable if not always gay, for we are not masters of gaiety to have it when we wish, but we are inexcusable if we are not always good, tractable, and obliging, for we have it in the power of our will to be so; and all that is required is to resolve to overcome our contrary humors and inclinations.

I certainly do not know why souls that have given themselves up to the divine goodness should not be always joyful; for is there any happiness equal to theirs? I would wish that we could sing everywhere. The imperfections you fall into ought not to trouble you; for you do not wish to cherish them, or to rest your affections in them. Remain then in peace, and live in meekness and humility of heart.

What a happiness to belong entirely to God! For He loves His own, He protects them, He conducts them, He brings them into the harbor of a desirable eternity. Remain then thus, and never permit your soul to be saddened, or to be in bitterness or scrupulosity, since He who loved it, and who died to make it live, is so good, so sweet, so amiable.[2]

---

2 "It is only the devil and the damned that ought to be sad, because their lot is decided for eternity, and their misfortune is beyond resource. Sinners obstinate in guilt will share the same fate; and, if there is sadness on earth, it is with them, since they take Hell for their portion."—*P. Lombez.*

CHAPTER TWENTY-ONE

REMEDIES FOR A BAD SADNESS[1]

FIRST REMEDY: We must receive sadness with patience, as a just punishment for our past vain gladness and joy; for the devil, seeing that we turn it to our profit, will not press it much upon us, and so long as we preserve a willingness not to be delivered, except according to the good pleasure of God, our patience will not fail to serve as a remedy.

Second remedy: We must sharply contradict the inclinations of sadness, and repel its suggestions, and, while it

---

1 "Were anyone to ask me how a sad soul may be delivered from interior suffering, I would answer by an example. There was a servant of God, a friend of the eternal wisdom, who, in the beginning of his conversion, was subject to fits of deep melancholy; not only did he lose all relish for reading and prayer, but he found it impossible to work. One day, as he sat in his chamber, abandoned to dejection, he heard an interior voice, which said to him: 'Why remain thus, sad and doing nothing? Why be consumed and wasted in the anguish of melancholy? Take courage, arise, do violence to thyself, meditate on My Passion and cruel sufferings, and thou wilt overcome thy grief.' The servant of God obeyed; meditation on the Passion of Jesus Christ banished his sadness, and by continuing in this holy exercise, he cured his soul, and was never more subject to melancholy."—*Bl. Suso.*

appears that everything we do then is done sadly, we must not discontinue our affairs; for the enemy, who desires by sadness to make us relent in the performance of good works, seeing that he gains nothing, but that, on the contrary, our works are better done, being done with reluctance, will soon cease to afflict us any longer.

Third remedy: When one is able, it is not amiss to sing some spiritual songs; for the devil has often been made by such means, on some account or other, to abandon his operations. Witness the spirit that agitated Saul, which was quieted by the sacred music of the harp.

Fourth remedy: It is good to employ oneself in some external occupation, and to diversify it as much as possible in order to preserve the mind from intense application to any sad object; to purify and warm the spirits, or, as we say, to raise them, sadness being a passion of a cold and humid character.[2]

Fifth remedy: Perform some exterior acts of piety, though you do so without any relish, such as embracing the crucifix, pressing it to your breast, or kissing the hands and feet, raising your hands and eyes to Heaven, uttering some words of love and confidence like these: "My Well-Beloved is all mine, and I am all His; my Beloved is a bouquet of myrrh on my heart. My eyes are wearied looking up on high; my God, I will never cease to say: when wilt Thou comfort me?

---

2   "Take a walk on beautiful days, in places where the air is pure, and where the sight of nature will enchant the imagination, and drive far away those dark and dismal images which real evils, or, more dangerous still, the melancholy humor, had impressed upon it.

   "A walk, with the elasticity of the air, sets the blood and other fluids in motion, refines and purifies the humors; the powers of our body resume their natural play, everything takes back its tone; melancholy is dissipated, and joy returns."—*P. Lombez.*

O Jesus, be a Jesus to me. Live Jesus! And may my soul live! Who will separate me from the love of my God?" And other like things.

Sixth remedy: A moderate discipline is sometimes good, because the voluntary affliction of the exterior impetrates interior consolation for the soul, and while applying pains to the body without, we feel less the effect of those within, according to that which the Psalmist says: "But as for me, when He afflicted me, I clothed myself with haircloth." And elsewhere, perhaps to the same purpose: "Thy rod and Thy staff have comforted me."

Seventh remedy: Prayer is the sovereign remedy, according to the expression of St. James: "If anyone be sad, let him pray." I do not mean that we must employ our time of prayer in long meditations, but I mean that, during it, we must make frequent petitions to God; we must always then address His divine goodness in invocations full of confidence, which we are apt to forget when in joy, and likewise, when free from trouble, imagining that there is no longer any need to excite sentiments of fear in our hearts; for example, such as these: "O Lord, most just and terrible, O! How I tremble before Thy sovereign majesty!" and the like. But in times of sadness, we must employ words of sweetness; for example: "O God of mercy most good and most gracious, Thou art my heart, my joy, my hope, the dear spouse of my soul," and the like; and we must employ them, whether sadness likes it or not, giving it no audience or credit when endeavoring to prevent us from uttering these words of confidence and love; and though we seem to do so without fruit, we must not cease to expect the fruit, which will not fail to appear after a little perseverance.[3] Frequent Communion is also an excellent means of banishing sadness, for this heavenly bread strengthens the heart and rejoices the mind by giving us the Master of consolations.

Eighth remedy: One of the safest remedies is to discover our heart, without concealing anything, to some prudent and spiritual person, mentioning to him the resentments, attachments, and suggestions that proceed from our sadness, and the reasons with which we entertain them; and all this humbly and faithfully. The first condition that the devil imposes on a soul which he wishes to afflict and seduce, is silence, just as the seditious do in conspiracies, for they require above all things that their undertakings and resolutions should be kept secret. God, on the contrary, requires discretion as the first condition; not wishing indeed that we should indiscreetly discover His graces and favors, but that we should make them known with prudence, and according to the rules of an humble discretion, to persons endowed with the requisite qualities.

But, in fine, if you do not find repose in these remedies, have patience; wait till the sun rises, it will dissipate the mist; have good courage, *this sickness will not be to death, but that God may be glorified by it.* Act like those who feel their stomach sick and disordered at sea; for, after

---

3   "Prayer, which is the greatest remedy for all evils, is singularly the remedy we should employ against sadness. The Apostle St. James points it out to us: *If there be anyone sad among you,* he says, *let him have recourse to prayer.* Our soul cannot communicate with God, but the sight of this ravishing object will carry it into joy, and make it share in the divine happiness. Having promised to grant us all that we ask of Him with the requisite conditions, how can He reject a prayer so legitimate as that of dissipating the sadness which Hell has breathed into our hearts, which is the mortal poison of our souls, and which hinders us from contemplating Him, from loving Him, and from tasting Him as He desires?"—*P. Lombez.*

they have tumbled about, both in mind and body, through the whole vessel, in order to find some alleviation, they at last take hold of the mast, and embrace it as fast as possible in order to be secure against the turnings which they experience in their head: it is true, their comfort is brief and uncertain. But if, with humility, you embrace the foot of the cross, when you cannot find a remedy anywhere else, you will at least find patience there sweeter than elsewhere, and trouble less disagreeable.

Rejoice as much as you can in doing good; for it is a double grace in good works, to be well done and to be joyfully done.[4] And when I say: in doing good, I do not mean to say that when you fall into some defect, you should abandon yourself to sadness on that account; no, in the name of God, for that would be to add defect to defect; but I mean to say that you should persevere in wishing to do good, and that you should always return to good as soon as you know you have departed from it, and that, by means of this fidelity, you should live for the most part joyfully.

In fine, we should belong to God without reserve, without division, without exception, and without any

---

4 "If Jesus Christ, our Divine Master, never laughed, it was because the plenitude of His perfections placed Him above all human imperfections; and laughter is one of them, but inseparable from our condition. God does not condemn it, because we are neither gods nor angels. Laughter proceeds from a sudden joy caused by the sight or thought of some object agreeable and new, or newly remembered; hence our Divine Saviour, to whom all things were continually present, was not susceptible of that sudden joy which novelty causes. Moreover, His soul, enjoying continually the beatific vision, was capable only of sentiments divinely-human; so that if He never laughed, neither was He ever sad, according to the words of the prophet Isaias: *Non erit tristis neque turbulentus.* If on the eve of His Passion He said that He was overwhelmed with a mortal sadness, this ought to be understood only of the impression of sadness on the imagination and on the senses, and not of sadness itself, of which His ever-blessed soul was incapable."—*P. Lombez.*

other pretensions than the honor of being His. If we had a single thread of affection in our heart that did not belong to Him, O God! We ought this very instant to tear it away. Let us then remain in peace, and say with the great lover of the cross: "Let no one come to disturb me; for, as for me, I carry in my heart the stigmata of my Jesus." Yes, my dearest daughter, if we knew a single piece of our heart not to be marked with the stamp of the crucifix, we should not wish to retain it for one moment. What good is there in being disquieted? *My soul, hope in God; why art thou sad, and why dost thou trouble me,* since God is my God, and my heart is a heart entirely His?[5]

---

5   God wishes to be served with joy. This is the glory and pleasure of good masters; the sadness and sorrow of servants dishonor and disgrace their masters.

CHAPTER TWENTY-TWO

CONSOLATIONS IN SUFFERINGS

LET us cast ourselves at the foot of the crucifix, and consider our pains in comparison with the cross and the injuries which Our Lord endured: by this means the heaviness of our afflictions will appear light and little, and sometimes so agreeable that we shall far prefer suffering to the enjoyment of any other consolation, separated from suffering. Alas! When we see our Saviour, after a thousand opprobriums, crucified and dead amid thorns and nails, and near Him Our Lady and St. John in the midst of the wonderful and terrible darkness that happened during His Passion, we should say that, without a doubt, crosses and afflictions are more amiable than contentments and delights; inasmuch as the Wisdom of God chose them for Himself and for His truest and most beloved servants. Ah! How great a grace it ought to be for us to be a little crucified with Our Lord, and to be able to testify our love

towards Him in the midst of tribulations, as He testified
His love towards us during His Passion![1]

The remedies prescribed by physicians, and the medi-
cines presented by apothecaries, are often rejected by the
sick, but being offered by some beloved hand, love over-
comes horror, and they are received with joy. Here is a little
sick child, that, without seeing its mother, and merely from
the knowledge it has of her will, takes everything brought to
it, and uses food without any pleasure, for it has no pleasure
in eating, nor has it the contentment of seeing its mother,
but it eats and drinks simply to do her will. My God, why
in like manner does not the good pleasure of Our Lord
make bitterness amiable, pain delightful, and agony desirable to us, when God seems to be gratified with it?

Mystic bees make their most excellent honey in the
wounds of the lion of the tribe of Juda, slaughtered, rent,
and torn in pieces on Mount Calvary; and the children of
the cross glory in their admirable riddle which the world
cannot understand; from death, which devours all, comes
forth the meat of our consolation, and from death, stronger than all, comes forth the sweetness of the honey of
our love.

Let us then unite our pains with the torments of Jesus
Christ, that the former may be enriched by the value and
merit of the latter, and let us believe that our sufferings can

---

1 "The soldier is too cowardly who wishes to remain always in the shade, and it is
rather delicate a thing to wish to live at one's ease both in this world and the next. It
is written: *Woe to you who laugh, for you shall one day weep!* Be not astonished then, O
Christian, if Jesus Christ gives you a share in His sufferings, that He may give you a
share in His glory, and if He allows you to feel some of the many thorns that pierced
His head. Is it to be maltreated, to be treated like Jesus Christ? or is it not the greatest
misfortune, to be left in repose?"—*Bossuet.*

never, either in quantity or in quality, be compared with those of Our Lord and His saints; never can we suffer anything for Him in comparison with that which He has suffered for us.[2]

This is the motive which made the saints receive the affronts, calumnies, and opprobriums that the world heaped on them, as an extreme favor and a singular honor; hence they gloried in their crucifix and in the annihilation of themselves, having more content, joy, glory, and felicity on the throne of the cross, than ever Solomon had on his throne of ivory, and their love was so strong and so powerful that the waters of tribulation and rivers of persecution could not extinguish it.

The virtues that spring up in the midst of prosperity are usually slender and weak, and those that grow in the midst of adversity are strong and robust, just as we see that the best vines grow among stones.[3]

I beg of God that He may be always in the midst of your heart, that it may not be moved by every wind, and that, giving you a share of His cross, He may communicate

---

2   St. Ludwina furnishes us with an admirable example of this resignation. She suffered the most cruel pains for thirty-eight years, obliged to remain continually in bed. Yet, when her sufferings were at the worst, she thus sweetly addressed herself to God: "O my Lord, may I receive in good part the strokes of Thy hand, and may I be content to see that Thou dost not spare my body from pains, for it is a great mark that Thou hast some good design over me! I am like a little clay, O my Creator! In Thy divine hands; give me then, I beg of Thee, the shape Thou judgest proper, for Thy glory and for my salvation, and do not fear to meet with any resistance in me."

3   All the saints have acknowledged, after St. Paul, that a body full of health and without suffering, is a great obstacle to sanctity. The seal, says St. Diadochus in his *Treatise on Perfection,* cannot lay its impress on wax that is as hard as a stone; we must of necessity soften the wax at the fire. In like manner, God can scarcely lay the impress of His perfections on a soul that is not prepared, and, as it were, softened by infirmities of body; for health and prosperity make it hard against the touches of grace, while sorrows soften it.

to you His holy patience and divine love, which render tribulations so precious.

Keep a holy silence, for truly it is good to spare our words for God and for His glory. God has held you by His good hand in your affliction. But, moreover, dear daughter, we must act thus always. "My God!" said St. Gregory to an afflicted bishop, "how is it possible that our hearts, which have been elevated to Heaven, can ever be disturbed by the occurrences of earth?" This was well said: the very sight of our dear Jesus crucified can sweeten in one moment all our sorrows, which are only flowers in comparison with His thorns. And since our grand rendezvous is eternity, what is the value of anything that passes with time?

Consider that this mortal life is full of trials to which everyone is subject, that consolations are rare and labors innumerable, and therefore that we are in a state in which we must expect more of the bread of bitterness than honey, with the assurance, nevertheless, that He for whom we suffer and for whom we have resolved to nourish holy patience in the midst of opposition, will in due season bestow on us the consolations of His Holy Spirit; changing the nails and thorns of contradiction into a collection of precious pearls for eternity, and giving at the same time a new luster and splendor to our charity. We are told of a fire which wonderfully burns in water; in like manner, holy charity is so strong that it nourishes its flames amid the waters of adversity.

Let us represent to ourselves the crown of Heaven, which is not given without victory, and victory, which is not given without war; we shall then regard the combat of tribulation as agreeable. Ah! If we lifted up our eyes to Heaven, we should see that not one of the mortals who are now immortal there, arrived in it by any other way than that of continual trouble and affliction: why then do we complain of the little difficulties which God sends us, and fail in patience for a trifle, when the smallest drop of humility would suffice to make us support patiently that which happens to us justly for our sins?[4]

When He places before our eyes some pains, labors, and dangers, to which we are of necessity compelled to submit, let us immolate ourselves in spirit to the good pleasure of God, and tenderly kiss this cross, remembering the general consolation that is to be found in almost all the evils of this life, namely, the hope that they will not be permanent, and that we shall soon see their end. Then let us cry out from the depth of our heart, in imitation of St. Andrew: "We hail thee, O precious cross; we hail thee, O blessed tribulation; how amiable thou art, O holy affliction, descended from the amiable bosom of the Father of eternal mercy, and destined for us from all eternity!"

The only cure for most of our maladies and infirmities, whether corporal or spiritual, is patience and conformity to the will of God, resigning ourselves to His good

---

4 "Formerly, under the law of Moses, the Lord promised the fruits of the earth to those who should walk in His commandments. On the contrary, since delivering Himself to the death of the cross, as a voluntary victim, He wishes that we should believe, in opposition to our senses, that sufferings are a favor, and persecutions a reward. All do not understand this word; but let him who has ears to hear, hear; and let him whose heart is opened to the Gospel, understand these truths, and adore their salutary rigor.

"Great prosperity is usually a punishment, and chastisements are favors. For what son is there, says the Apostle, whose father does not correct him? The Lord mercifully chastises the children whom He loves. Persevere, then, under His discipline. If He spares you the rod and correction, fear lest He reserves you for torment."—*Bossuet.*

pleasure without reserve or exception, in health, in sickness, in contempt, in honor, in consolation, in desolation, in time, and in eternity; willingly accepting every trouble both of mind and body from His most amiable hand, as if we saw it present; even offering ourselves to endure more, if it should seem good to Him. No one can tell how pure and meritorious such an acceptance of the divine will renders our sufferings, when we not only receive them with meekness and patience, but cherish them, love them, and caress them, on account of the divine good pleasure from which they proceed.

As a branch of *agnus-castus* drives away weariness from the traveler who carries it, so the cross, the mortification, the yoke, the law of the Saviour, who is the true Chaste Lamb, is a burden which refreshes, solaces, and recreates those hearts that love His Divine Majesty. There is no labor in that which is loved; or, if there be labor, it is a beloved labor: labor blended with holy love is a kind of bittersweet more agreeable to the taste than pure sweetness.

Are you aware of what shepherds in Arabia do when they perceive the approach of thunder and lightning? They retire under the laurel trees, both themselves and their flocks. When we observe that persecutions and contradictions threaten us with some great annoyance, we must take shelter, both we and our afflictions, under the holy cross, by a true confidence that all will turn to the good of those who love God.

Keep up your heart then; remove anxieties; often cast your confidence on the Providence of Our Lord; and be assured that heaven and earth will sooner pass away than that Our Lord will fail to protect you, so long as you are His obedient child, or at least desirous to be so. Two or three times a day examine whether your heart is not disquieted about something, and finding that it is, endeavor upon the spot to reinstate it in repose.

Chapter Twenty-Three

The Cross of the Good Thief

SOLOMON says that all that passes under the sun is vanity and affliction of spirit. There is no man under the sun who can avoid the cross and sufferings; but the wicked sinners are, contrary to their liking and in spite of their will, fastened to the cross and to tribulations, and by their impatience render their crosses hurtful; they have sentiments of esteem for themselves, like those of the bad thief; by this means they unite their crosses with that of this wicked man, and infallibly their reward will be the same.

The good thief transformed a bad cross into a cross of Jesus Christ. Certainly the fatigues, the injuries, the tribulations that we receive are thieves' crosses, and we have well deserved them; we ought then to say humbly with the good thief: "We receive in our sufferings that which we have deserved by our sins." It is thus we shall, by our humility, render our thief's cross the cross of a true Christian. Let us, then, like the good thief, unite our sinner's cross with the cross of Him who has saved us; and by this loving and devout union of our sufferings with the sufferings and cross of Jesus Christ, we shall enter, like so many good thieves, into His friendship and company in Paradise.

CHAPTER TWENTY-FOUR

THE CROSSES OF PROVIDENCE
ARE THE MOST AGREEABLE TO GOD

"IF ANYONE will come after Me," says Our Lord, "let him take up his cross and follow Me." To take up one's cross cannot mean anything else than that we should receive and suffer all the pains, contradictions, afflictions, and mortifications that happen to us in this life, without any exception, with an entire submission and indifference.

Let us often immolate our heart to the love of Jesus, even on the altar of the cross, where He immolated His for the love of us. The cross is the royal gate by which we enter into the temple of sanctity; he who seeks for it elsewhere, will not find a trace of it.

The best crosses are the weightiest, and the weightiest are those which we receive most reluctantly, according to the inferior portion of the soul. The crosses we meet with in the street are excellent, and still more those we find in the house, and in proportion as they are more teasing, they are better; they are of much greater value than disciplines, fasts, and everything else that austerity has invented. Here, indeed, appears the generosity of the children of the cross, and of the inhabitants of the sacred mount of Calvary.

The crosses we impose on ourselves are always put on in a mincing kind of way, because they are our own, and therefore they are less meritorious. Humble yourself, and receive those joyfully that are imposed on you without your selection. The length of the cross much increases its value; be faithful unto death, and you shall have the crown of life. You are fond of the crucifix; what then would you wish to be, unless crucified?

Our Lord gave David his choice of the rod with which he should be scourged: and God be praised! But it appears to me that I would not have chosen; I would have left it all to His Divine Majesty. The more a cross is from God, the more we ought to love it.

Let us receive with love the crosses that we have not chosen, that God gives us from His hand; let us bless them, let us love them: they are all perfumed with the excellent odor of the place from which they come. Where there is less of our own choice, there is more of the good pleasure of God. I infinitely prefer the evil that comes to us from our Heavenly Father before that which comes to us from our own will.

Our Lord has well shown us that it is not necessary we should choose our crosses, but that it is necessary we should take and carry such as are presented to us; for when He was about to die, in order to redeem us, and satisfy the will of His Heavenly Father, He did not choose His cross, but humbly received that which the Jews had prepared for Him.

I particularly love the evil that the sole choice of our Heavenly Father sends us, and much prefer it to that which we might select ourselves.

Behold true virtue, and how it ought to be practiced. Seneca showed it a long time ago in a beautiful expression; I wish it were St. Augustine who had uttered the words: "The perfection of man consists in suffering all things well, as if they happened to him of his own choice."

To suffer for God is to fill our hands with the purest and most precious gold wherewith to purchase Heaven. A single package, if I may so speak, of this divine gold, suffices to put us in possession of the glory of Paradise. "A moment of light tribulation," says St. Paul, "worketh for us an immense weight of glory." The same observation hardly applies to our ordinary actions; we may say that the most virtuous, compared with afflictions, are only common money, a gross metal. A great deal of such is required to procure anything of value, and it often happens that such money is counterfeit, because, in most of our good works, our self-love enters, and alters their purity.

Christian perfection consists in suffering well. To acquire solid virtues, complain not of your pains. Endure contradictions patiently. God gives you an occasion of practicing patience; would you wish to let it escape? Perhaps in your life, you will never meet the like of it again; perhaps it may be the last service you will render to His

Divine Majesty. Be constant, and He will bless you in your affliction.[1]

Let us love our crosses; seen with the eyes of love, they are all of gold, and though Our Lord is dead there in the midst of nails and thorns, there is found in the cross a collection of precious pearls that will compose our crown of glory if we courageously carry our crown of thorns. The time of afflictions and contradictions is the beautiful harvest time, when the soul gathers in the richest benedictions of Heaven; one day then is more profitable than six at another time. Let us, therefore, be always fastened to the cross, and let a hundred thousand arrows transpierce our flesh, provided the inflamed dart of the love of God has previously penetrated our heart, and let this divine wound make us die of its holy death, which is more precious than a thousand lives. In what can we testify our love towards Him who suffered so much for us, if not in the midst of contradictions, repugnances, and aversions? Let us cast ourselves upon the thorns of difficulties, let us allow our heart to be transfixed with the lance of contradictions, let us drink the vinegar and gall of temporal afflictions, since our sweet Saviour wishes it to be so; as the flowers grow among thorns, so divine love increases better in the midst of tribulation than in the midst of comfort.[2]

---

1 All the sufferings of this life are not worthy to be compared with the immense weight of glory that is prepared for you. Have courage, then: when evils are greatest and most desperate, they are nearest their end. Cease not to suffer. The time is short. We must complete that which is wanting in us, to the Passion of Jesus Christ.

2 We must ask to know how to suffer well, since we ought to profit by the grave lessons which suffering gives: its first is obedience. St. Teresa always obeyed, even when her directors contended with the Spirit of God within her; she was submissive, because she had suffered much and well. We must be kind towards suffering: it is a faithful and devoted friend, that brings us true blessings; it gives us solid virtue, which

Oh! How happy are the souls that, to acquire love, drink courageously the chalice of sufferings with Our Lord, mortify themselves, carry their cross, and suffer and receive willingly from His divine hand every kind of occurrence with submission to His good pleasure! But, my God, how few there are who do these things as they ought! We meet often enough with souls who desire to suffer and to carry the cross, and I know there are some who even ask afflictions from God, but it is on condition that He will frequently visit and console them in their pains and sufferings, and that He will show them that He is much pleased with their sufferings, and intends to reward them with eternal glory. There are also many who desire, like the two disciples, to know the degree of glory they shall have in Heaven; certainly, this desire is rather impertinent; for we should never, in any manner, inquire into that, but occupy ourselves always in serving His Divine Majesty as faithfully as we can, observing His divine commandments, His counsels, and His wishes most exactly, and with as much perfection, purity, and love as will be possible for us, leaving the care of the rest to His infinite goodness, who will not fail, if we do our duty, to reward us with immortal and incomprehensible glory, by giving Himself to us: so much account does He make of what we do for Him. In a word, He is a good master; we must endeavor to be good and faithful servants to Him, and He will not fail to be a faithful remunerator. Oh! If we knew what a happiness it is to faithfully serve the Divine Saviour of our souls, and to drink of His chalice

---

detaches us from everything. And, besides, when we suffer, we easily humble and abase ourselves."—*Père de Ravignan.*

with Him, oh! How willingly we would embrace pains and
sufferings, after the example of the great St. Catherine of
Siena, who preferred the crown of thorns to that of gold!
Thus we ought to act; for, in fine, the way of the cross and
of affliction is a secure way, and one that leads us straight to
God, and to the perfection of His love. If we are faithful to
drink courageously of His chalice, crucifying ourselves with
Him in this life, His divine goodness will not fail to glorify
us eternally in the next.[3]

---

3   "There are many afflictions that purify man and conduct him to supreme felicity, did
he but know how to use them well. God often sends us cruel afflictions without their
being deserved; He wishes to prove our constancy, and to show us that we are nothing
of ourselves. We have proofs of this in the Old Testament. Sometimes He sends them
to manifest His glory, as we see in the Gospel in the case of the man born blind: Our
Lord declared, when restoring sight to him, that the man was innocent. Some are
struck because they deserve it, as happened to the thief crucified with Jesus Christ;
the Saviour promised him eternal life, because he was converted on the cross. Others
have not deserved what they suffer, but God wishes to purify them from some faults,
to correct their pride, and to humble them by exposing them to injustice.

"There are other afflictions which God permits of His goodness, because they
preserve those who suffer them from greater misfortunes. Some make their Purgatory here, in sickness, poverty, and adversity, and thus avoid far greater pains; others
are a target for the persecutions of the wicked, and, at the hour of their death, God
spares them from the assaults of the devils; others, in fine, are tormented by violent
passions."—Bl. Suso.

CHAPTER TWENTY-FIVE

THE BEST CROSSES

LET us, I pray, slightly unmask an error that is found in the minds of many, who do not value or wish to carry the crosses that are presented to them, unless they are rough and heavy. For example, a religious will willingly submit to practice great austerities, to fast, to wear the hair-cloth, to take severe disciplines, and he will have a repugnance to obey when commanded not to fast, or even to take some rest, and such other things, in which he seems to have more satisfaction than pain. Now, you deceive yourself, if you imagine that there is less virtue in overcoming yourself in these things than in things more difficult; for the merit of the cross does not lie in its weight, but in the manner of carrying it. I will go further, and say, that there is sometimes more merit in carrying a cross of straw than a very heavy one, because the lighter crosses are, and the more contemptible, the less conformable are they to our inclinations, which always look to show. And it is a thing most certain that there is always more virtue in not saying a word that has been forbidden us by our superiors, or even in not raising our eyes to look upon something which we are very anxious to see, and the like, than in wearing the haircloth, because when we have put this on our back, there is no need of thinking any more about it. But in these petty practices we must have a continual attention over ourselves, to guard against falling into imperfection.

Now, then, you see very well that the word of Our Lord, which orders you to take up your cross, ought to be understood of receiving readily and indifferently all the obediences that are given you, and all the mortifications and contradictions that you meet with, though they should be light and of little importance, assured as you ought to be, that the merit of the cross does not lie in its weight, but in the perfection with which it is carried.

Truly it is good to mortify one's flesh, but it is especially necessary to purify our affections and to renovate our hearts. God says to us: "Rend and tear your hearts, for it is against them My anger is provoked." This is what we do by these little mortifications, frequently repeated and faithfully practiced: to suffer a little rebuke in a spirit of meekness, to act through obedience when we feel much repugnance in doing so, not to complain when we imagine there is great reason why we should, to endure the defects of those with whom we live. It is on these occasions that we must rend our hearts, and make a continual sacrifice of our own wills, our natural inclinations, and give some proofs to God of our love and our fidelity.[1]

---

1   "God has the goodness to put some of our Purgatory into each day; let us accept,

O God! You will tell me, this is a great renunciation, and it is necessary to be very attentive over oneself not to follow one's own will, and not to seek that which our self-love desires; for it has many artifices to deceive us, and to turn our attention off ourselves. That is true, but there is a remedy. Remember that Our Lord directs us to take up our cross and to follow Him. He says our own cross; which I mention in order to prevent the extravagances of many, who, when someone mortifies them a little, are vexed and annoyed, saying that if such or such a thing had happened to them, or what has happened to another, they would have endured it willingly; and in like manner with sicknesses, for they wish to have that which God has given to another, and not that which He has sent them Himself for their good. That is not to carry our cross as Our Lord wishes us to carry it, and as He has taught us by His example. If then we wish to carry our cross after Him, we must imitate Him by receiving indifferently whatever happens to us, without choice or exception.[2]

Often in spirit kiss the crosses which Our Lord Himself

---

embrace the cross which is presented to us. Let us take care not to complain, nor to imagine that suffering is a new invention. A person might easily suppose it was, on seeing our astonishment, and hearing our murmurs. The saints, crushed and ground down by trials of all sorts, seized on suffering as gold from the mine.

"See how the gold taken from the earth is cast into a crucible; had the gold thought and speech, it would cry out: I suffer, take me out of this. And yet this gold is purified, and soon it will shine on the brows of kings, and on the altars of the living God. The cross effects the same in our regard; it is our crucible."—*P. De Ravignan.*

2 "We do not know how to love our well-beloved Saviour, no, we do not know how to love Him. Do you require a proof of it? Let us suppose that Our Lord Jesus Christ had not come to suffer and to die on the earth—would there be much change required in our mode of existence, and in our ideas, in order to remove that which is now conformable to His example and His doctrine? Alas, no; we might continue to act as we act; we should have the same aversion for suffering, the same horror of contempt. Is this, then, to love Thee, my beloved Saviour? No, a thousand times, no!"—*P. De Ravignan.*

lays upon your shoulders. Do not look to see whether they are made of a precious or a perfumed wood; they better deserve the name of crosses when they are made of mean, common, worm-eaten wood. I assure you this thought is ever returning to my mind, and I know only this refrain; undoubtedly it is the canticle of the Lamb; it is a little sad, but it is melodious and beautiful: "My Father, not as I will, but as Thou wilt."

Magdalen sought Our Lord while holding Him; she asked Him of Himself; she did not see Him in the form in which she desired to see Him: on this account she was not content to see Him thus, and sought to find Him otherwise; she wished to see Him in His garments of glory, and not in the mean dress of a gardener; but at length she knew Him when He said: "Mary!"

Do you see, it is Our Lord in the dress of a gardener you meet with every day, here and there, in the various occasions of mortification that present themselves to you? You would much wish Him to offer you other more beautiful mortifications. O God! The most beautiful are not the best. Do you not think He says to you: Mary, Mary? Before you can see Him in His glory, He wishes to plant in your garden a great many little flowers, small but to His liking; and this is the reason why He is so clad. May our hearts be ever united to His, and our wills to His good pleasure!

CHAPTER TWENTY-SIX

_____

THE WOOD OF THE TRUE CROSS

HAPPY are those who suffer persecution for justice's sake; this beatitude, the last in order, is the first in Our Lord's esteem, and I often look upon it as the sovereign happiness of the present life. Those who are unjustly perse-cuted carry the resemblance of the Saviour better, and lead a life hidden with Jesus Christ in God: they appear wicked and they are good, dead and they are living, poor and they are rich, foolish and they are wise, detested before men and in benediction before God. Persecutions are pieces of the cross of Jesus Christ; we must not allow a particle of them to perish.[1]

_____

1 "The cross can take the place of everything, and nothing can take its place. He who suffers with patience has no need of any other means of salvation: provided he is in the state of grace, the cross holds the place of all, of great apostolic labors, of high gifts of prayer, of fasts, of haircloths, of alms, and of everything else most splendid that the saints have wrought; let us say still more: accompanied with a great love, it is of more value than all those things. But he who suffers nothing, were he to present to God and man the works of zeal of a St. Francis Xavier, the works of charity of a St. Vincent de Paul, and even greater, would be behind a poor sick patient, united

I saw, some time ago, a little girl carrying a pitcher of water on her head, and in the middle of it she had put a bit of wood. I wished to know why, and she said that it was to prevent the movement of the water, for fear it should be spilled. Then, henceforward, said I, we must put the cross in the middle of our hearts to prevent the movements of our affections in this wood and by this wood, in order that they may not spill over in uneasiness and trouble of mind.

To suffer is almost the only good we can do in this world; for rarely do we perform any good without mixing up some evil along with it. And, besides, Our Lord is never so near us as when we suffer something for His love.[2] He watches over us while we repose in peace upon His bosom, and makes us draw advantage from our tribulations.

On what occasions can we make great acts of the union of our heart with the will of God, of the mortification of our self-love, or of the love of our own abjection, in a word, of our crucifixion, unless during these rough and severe trials? Have I not often told you to divest yourself of all creatures in order to clothe yourself with our crucified Lord? Courage, then! It is Our Lord who wishes thus

---

to God, and further away from the conditions of salvation, whose foundation Jesus Christ has made the cross."—*P. Engelvin, Franciscan.*

2   "If we shall have anything to regret at the moment of death, it will be that the time of suffering for God has passed, and consequently the means of enriching ourselves are gone. The privilege of suffering is perhaps the only advantage we have above the angels. They may indeed be the companions of Our Lord, but they cannot be the companions of His death. Those blessed intelligences may well appear before the face of God, as victims burning with an ardent charity, but their impassible nature prevents them from giving one generous proof of their affection in the midst of anguish, or receiving that honor which is so sweet to him who loves, to love even to die, and even to die of love. Oh, how great a grace it is to love and to suffer, to love while suffering, and to suffer while loving! Let us never lose one of our crosses, but let us often say to ourselves: courage! the time of suffering is short, the love that suffering merits is eternal."—*Bossuet.*

to prove your heart. It is not severity, it is clemency. Have courage: provided that your heart is faithful to Him, He will not load you above your strength, and He will support your burden with you, when He sees that with a good affection you bow down your shoulders beneath the weight He lays upon you.[3]

Blessed are the crucified! In this world our inheritance is the cross, in the next it will be glory.

All is over. After the few days of this mortal life which remain to us, a boundless eternity will ensue. It matters little whether we are convenienced or inconvenienced here, provided that for all eternity we shall be happy and blessed. Let the thought of this holy eternity which awaits us, the thought of being a Christian, a child of Jesus Christ, regenerated in His blood, be your consolation; for in this alone lies our glory, that Jesus Christ has died for us.

---

3   "If the most ignorant men know the burdens that their poor horses or asses are able to carry, and do not put on too heavy a load for fear of overpowering them; if the potter knows how long the clay should remain in the furnace, in order to be heated to that degree which renders it fit for use, and does not leave it for a moment more or less; we cannot possibly have reflected, or we should not dare to say that God, who is wisdom itself, and who loves us with an infinite love, lays upon our shoulders a weight that is too heavy, or leaves us too long in the fire of tribulation. Let us then be without uneasiness. The fire will not be greater, nor of longer duration, than is required to heat our clay to the necessary degree."—*St. Ephrem.*

Chapter Twenty-Seven

Calumnies

BLESSED *are they who suffer persecution for justice' sake,* because their life is hidden with Jesus Christ in God, and made conformable to His image, since He was during His whole life persecuted for justice, which, nevertheless, He fulfilled in the most perfect manner. Those who are unjustly persecuted by men are hidden in the secret of God's countenance; they are in detestation before men, but in benediction before God, to whom they are the odor of life unto life.

"Blessed are ye," says Our Lord, "when men shall speak all that is evil against you, untruly, for My sake." "If the world," says St. Paul, "did not find anything to say against us, we should not be truly the servants of God." Care not for human judgment, and you will have interior peace.

Disquiet not yourself about that which the world will say of you; await the judgment of God, and you will then judge those who now judge you. Think of Him for whom you labor, and they who would endeavor to cause you pain will not disturb you in the least. It is only amid the rocks that the waves raise noise and froth.

It is said that those who use the preservative called "the charm of St. Paul" do not swell, if bitten and stung by a viper, provided the medicine be of good quality; in like manner, when humility and meekness are good and true, they secure us against that inflation and ardor which injuries are accustomed to provoke in our hearts. And if, being stung and bitten by slanderers and enemies, we become fierce, enraged, and spiteful, this is an evident sign that our humility and meekness are not true and sincere, but false and artificial.

If the world contemn[1] us, let us rejoice; for it has reason, since we acknowledge candidly that we are contemptible. If it esteem us, let us contemn its esteem and its judgment; for it is blind. Inquire little of that which the world thinks, put yourself to no trouble about it; let us despise its praise and its dispraise, and let us allow it to say whatever it pleases, whether good or bad.

To say that you are not what the world thinks, when it thinks well of you, is indeed good; for the world is a charlatan; it always says too much of everything, whether well of it, or ill of it. I find no better remedy in contradictions than to take no notice of them, not to speak of them, and to observe a great meekness towards the person who causes them. What do we gain by opposing the winds and the waves, but to be covered with dust and foam?

---

1   Contemn—that is, hold in contempt.—*Publisher*, 2013.

I only wish for reputation inasmuch as it is necessary for the service of God; provided that God is served, what matters it about good or bad renown, the splendor or disrepute of one's character?

My God! What is this reputation to which so many persons sacrifice themselves, as to an idol? It is a dream, a shadow, an opinion, a smoke, a praise whose memory perishes with the sound, an esteem which is often so false that many wonder at seeing themselves praised for virtues, knowing that they practice the opposite vices, and, on the other hand, blamed for vices which are not at all in them. Those who complain of lies are certainly delicate; these are a little cross of words which the air carries away. The saying, *he has stung me,* for *he has spoken ill of me,* displeases me; for there is much difference between the humming of a bee and its sting; a person must have an ear and a skin very tender indeed, if one cannot bear the tread of a fly, and the other is stung by its buzz.

We must take pleasure in being censured, because if we do not deserve it in one manner, we deserve it in another.

The life of good people is a mixture of sweetness and bitterness, and the hearts of the servants of God are like anvils, destined to be struck, and which live, nevertheless, by blows and outrages.

With the help of God, I shall never allow the maxim to depart from my mind, that *we must not live according to human prudence, but according to the laws of the Gospel;* for human prudence is genuine silliness. Oh, may God be pleased ever to defend us from it and make us continually live according to the spirit of the Gospel, which is sweet, simple, and amiable, teaching us to return good for evil!

Those were far advanced in the prudence of the flesh who manufactured this proverb: "a good name is better than a strong boundary wall," preferring reputation to riches, that is to say, vanity to avarice. O God! How far was that idea removed from the spirit of faith! Was there ever a reputation so torn asunder as that of Jesus Christ? With what injuries was He not attacked? With what calumnies was He not assailed? Yet the Eternal Father gave Him a name above all names, and exalted Him so much the more as He had been humbled. And did not the Apostles depart joyful from the assemblies in which they had received affronts for the name of Jesus?

Oh, yes! It is a glory to suffer in so worthy a cause. I understand it well; we would only wish for illustrious persecutions, that our light might shine in the midst of darkness, and our vanity sparkle through our sufferings; we would desire to be gloriously crucified. But when the martyrs suffered so many cruel torments, were they praised by the spectators? On the contrary, were they not cursed, and abandoned to execration? Ah! There are few people who wish to make mere rubbish, as it were, of their reputation, in order to procure the glory of Him who died so ignominiously upon the cross, that He might conduct us to a glory which will never end! If the grace of God has placed any justice in me, I ought to desire that on the day of Judgment, when the secrets of hearts will be manifested, there should be no one but God alone to know my justice, and that my injustices should be made known to all creatures.

Persecutions are pieces of the cross of Jesus Christ; we should scruple very much to allow the smallest particle of them to perish.

In what would we wish, I ask, to testify our love for Him who suffered so much for us if not in contradictions, repugnances, and aversions? Ah! Let our hearts be transpierced by the lance of opposition, let us eat the bread of bitterness and drink the vinegar of adversity, since our sweet Saviour wishes it to be so.

The Lord is the mirror of our soul, and the immovable pillar round which our desires revolve. This being so, let the heavens take up arms, let the earth and the elements break out in mutiny, let all creatures make war upon me, I confide in God; and to be in peace, it suffices me to know that I am with Him and He is with me.

Let us always have our eyes fixed on Jesus Christ crucified, let us walk in His service with confidence and simplicity, but wisely and discreetly; He will be the protector of our name, and if He permit it to be taken from us, He will restore us a better, or make us profit by the loss in holy humility, of which a single ounce is better than a ton of honor. If we be blamed unjustly, let us peaceably oppose truth to calumny; if the censure continue, let us persevere in our humility. Commending thus our reputation with our soul, into the hands of God, we shall best secure it. Let us serve God through good and evil report, after the example of St. Paul, that we may be able to say: "O my God, for Thee I have supported this opprobrium, for Thee confusion has covered my face."

A little virtue acquired in the midst of contradictions,

reproaches, censures, and reprimands, is of much more value than a great deal acquired in another manner. Oh, how happy we are to have sworn an eternal fidelity to our Master! There is nothing required to please Him but to have patience, while living virtuously; for we shall meet with occasions enough of suffering.

Love Him well, my dear sister, in the retreats which you make to pray and to adore; love Him when you receive Him in Holy Communion; love Him when your heart is inundated with His holy consolations; but, above all, love Him when you meet with trials, aridities, and tribulations; for thus He loved you in Paradise, but He testified more love in your regard amid the scourges, the nails, the thorns, and the darkness of Calvary.

You ought, in consideration of these things, to receive sweetly and patiently the *ennuis* that befall you, and bear them for the love of Him who only permits them for your good.

Lift up your heart then frequently to God, ask His assistance, and place your principal consolation in the happiness of belonging to Him. Every matter of annoyance will appear to you little, when you remember that you have so kind a friend, so great a support, so excellent a refuge.

ADIEU

OF ST. FRANCIS DE SALES TO THE PIOUS READER

IT IS with all my heart, I say the word, "Adieu." To God (*A Dieu*) may you ever belong in this life, serving Him faithfully in the midst of the pains we all have in carrying our crosses, and in the immortal life, blessing Him eternally with all the celestial court. The greater good of our souls is to be with God; and the greatest good, to be with God alone.

He who is with God alone, is never sad, unless for having offended God, and his sadness then consists in a profound but tranquil and peaceful humility and submission, after which he rises again in the Divine Goodness, by a sweet and perfect confidence, without chagrin or vexation.

He who is with God alone seeks only God, and because God is no less in tribulation than in prosperity, he remains in peace during times of adversity.

He who is with God alone thinks often of Him in the midst of the occupations of this life.

He who is with God alone would be glad that everyone should know he wishes to serve God, and to be engaged in exercises suitable to keep him united to God.

Live then entirely to God; desire only to please Him, and to please creatures only in Him, and for Him. What greater blessing can I wish you? Thus, then, by this continual wish I make for your soul, I say: Adieu.

To God let us belong, without end, without reserve, without measure, as He is ours forever. May we always unite our little crosses with His great one!

To God let us live, and to God without anything more, since out of Him, and without Him, we seek for nothing: no, not even for ourselves, who, indeed, out of Him, and without Him, are only true nothings.

Adieu. I desire for you the abundance of Divine Love, which is and will be forever the only good of our hearts, given to us only for Him, who has given His Heart entirely to us.

Let Jesus be our crown! Let Mary be our hope! I am, in the name of the Son and the Mother,

Sincerely yours,

FRANCIS DE SALES

SUPPLEMENT

---

1. WE SHOULD NOT DESPAIR OF THE SALVATION OF ANY SINNER[1]

S T. FRANCIS de Sales, says the Bishop of Belley, never wished that the repentance of any sinner should be despaired of before his last breath, observing that this life was the way of our pilgrimage, in which those who walked might fall, and those who fell might, by grace, rise again, and, like the giants in the fable, they sometimes rose stronger than they had fallen, grace superabounding where sin had abounded.

He went still further; for, even after death, he did not wish that anyone should pass a bad judgment on those who had led a bad life, unless it regarded those of whose damnation we are assured by the truth of the Holy Scripture. Beyond this point, He would not allow anyone to seek to penetrate into the secrets of God, which are reserved to His wisdom.

---

1 We take this chapter from the *Spirit of St. Francis de Sales,* by Camus [Bishop of Belley].

His principal reason was, that, as the first grace of justification does not fall under the merit of any preceding work, so the last grace, which is that of final perseverance, is not given to any merit either. Besides, who has known the mind of the Lord, and who has been His counselor? For this reason, He wished that, even after the last breath, we should hope well of the deceased person, however sad an end he might have seemed to make, because we can only form very uncertain conjectures, founded on external appearances, in which the most experienced are often deceived.[2]

2. SENTIMENTS OF ST. FRANCIS DE SALES ON THE NUMBER OF THE ELECT

The extreme gentleness of St. Francis de Sales, says the Bishop of Belley, from whom we borrow this chapter, always led him to the mildest opinions, however little probability they carried. We were conversing one day, in company, on this dreadful word of the Gospel: "Many are called, but few are chosen." Someone remarked that the number of the elect was called a little flock, as that of fools, or of the reprobate, was called infinite, and such things. He answered that he thought very few Christians (he spoke of those in the true Church, out of which there is no salvation) would be damned; because, he said, having the root of the True Faith, sooner or later it usually yields its fruit,

---

2 We read the following passage in the *Life of Père De Ravignan:* "In certain deaths there are hidden mysteries of mercy and strokes of grace, in which the eye of man beholds only the strokes of justice. By the gleams of the last light, God reveals Himself to souls whose greatest misfortune was to have been ignorant of Him; and the last sigh, understood by Him who searches hearts, may be a groan that asks for pardon."

which is salvation, and from being dead, becomes living by charity.

And when asked what, then, was the meaning of this word of the Gospel concerning the small number of the elect, he said that in comparison with the rest of the world and with infidel nations, the number of Christians was very small, but that of this small number there would be very few lost, according to this remarkable sentence: "There is no damnation for those who are in Jesus Christ" (*Rom.* 8:1). Which, indeed, is to be understood of justifying grace;[3] but this grace is not separated from a faith living and animated by charity. Moreover, as He who gives the grace to begin, gives also the grace to perfect the undertaking, so it is credible that the vocation to Christianity, which is a work of God, is a perfect work, and conducts to the end of all consummation, which is glory.

I added another reason, and he was pleased with it: that the mercy of God being above all His works, and swimming over His justice, as oil over vinegar, there was every reason for trusting in His own natural disposition to pity and forgive, abundantly shown forth in the copious redemption of the Saviour; and there was no sign for believing that God would have commenced to erect the salvation of the true Christian by faith, which is its foundation, without proceeding with it to the end, which consists in charity.

This doctrine is of great consolation, provided it does not make us negligent in doing good; for, it is not enough to say with the ancients: *The temple of the Lord, the temple*

---

3 Justifying grace—that is, Sanctifying Grace.—*Publisher,* 2013.

of the Lord—the Church, the Church, I am in the bosom of the true Church. Since the Church is holy, and the pillar of truth, it is our duty to live holily, as well as to believe truly; for, to commit crimes in the house of God, is to defile His sanctuary, and to render oneself doubly guilty. And who is unaware that the servant who knew the will of his Master, and did not trouble himself to perform it, deserved a double chastisement?

We should fear, said St. Francis de Sales, the judgments of God, but without discouragement, and take courage at the sight of His mercies, but without presumption. Those who have an excessive and inordinate fear of being damned show plainly that they have great need of humility and submission. We must indeed abase, annihilate, lose ourselves, but this ought to be to gain, preserve, save ourselves. That humility which is prejudicial to charity, is assuredly a false humility. Such is that which leads to trouble, to discouragement, to despair; for it is contrary to charity, which, while commanding us *to work out our salvation with fear and trembling,* forbids us at the same time to diffide in the goodness of God, who desires the conversion and salvation of all.

3. THE SOULS IN PURGATORY

The opinion of St. Francis de Sales, says the Bishop of Belley, was that, from the thought of Purgatory, we should draw more consolation than pain. The greater number of those, he said, who fear Purgatory so much, do so in consideration of their own interests, and of the love they bear themselves rather than the interests of God, and this happens because those who treat of this place from the pul-pit usually speak of its pains, and are silent of the happiness and peace which are found in it.

No doubt the torments are so great that the greatest sufferings of this life cannot be compared with them; but still, the interior satisfaction there is such, that no enjoy-ment or prosperity on earth can equal it.

The souls in Purgatory are in a constant state of union with God.

They are perfectly submissive to His will, or, to speak better, their will is so transformed into the will of God, that they cannot wish for anything but what God wishes; in such a manner, that if Paradise were opened to them, they would rather precipitate themselves into Hell than appear before God with the stains which they still perceive on themselves.

They are purified voluntarily and lovingly, because such is the divine good pleasure. The souls in Purgatory are there indeed for their sins, sins which they have detested, and sovereignly detested; but as to the abjection and pain that still remain, of being detained there, and deprived for a time of the joy of the blessed in Paradise, they endure all that lovingly, and devoutly pronounce this canticle of the divine justice: "Thou art just, O Lord, and thy judgment is right."

They wish to be there in the manner that pleases God, and for as long a time as He pleases.

They are impeccable, and cannot have the least motion of impatience, or be guilty of the smallest imperfection.

They love God more than themselves, and more than

all things else, with a perfect, pure, and disinterested love.

They are consoled by angels.

They are assured of their salvation.

Their most bitter bitterness is in the most profound peace.

If Purgatory is a kind of Hell as regards pain, it is a kind of Paradise as regards the sweetness which charity diffuses through the heart—charity which is stronger than death, and more powerful than Hell, and whose lamps are fire and flames.

A state more desirable than terrible, since its flames are flames of love.

Terrible, nevertheless, since they postpone the end of all consummation, which consists in seeing and loving God, and in this vision and love, to praise and glorify Him for all eternity. With regard to this subject, St. Francis de Sales approved very much of the admirable *Treatise on Purgatory,* written by the blessed Catherine of Genoa.

If these things be so, I shall be asked, why recommend so much the souls in Purgatory to our charity?

The reason is, because, notwithstanding their advantages, the state of these souls is still very sad and truly deserving of compassion, and, moreover, the glory which they will render to God in Heaven is delayed. These two motives ought to engage us, by our prayers, our fasts, our alms, and all kinds of good works, especially by offering the Holy Sacrifice of the Mass for them, to procure their speedy deliverance.

When any of St. Francis de Sales' friends or acquaintances died, he never grew weary of speaking fondly of them, or recommending them to the prayers of others.

His usual expression was: "We do not remember sufficiently our dead, our faithful departed;" and the proof of it is, that we do not speak enough of them. We turn away from that discourse as from a sad subject, we leave the dead to bury their dead; their memory perishes from us with the sound of their mourning bell; we forget that the friendship which ends, even with death, is never true, Holy Scripture assuring us that true love is stronger than death.

He was accustomed to say that in this single work of mercy, the thirteen others are assembled.

Is it not, he said, in some manner, to visit the sick, to obtain by our prayers the relief of the poor suffering souls in Purgatory?

Is it not to give drink to those who thirst after the vision of God, and who are enveloped in burning flames, to share with them the dew of our prayers?

Is it not to feed the hungry, to aid in their deliverance by the means which faith suggests?

Is it not truly to ransom prisoners?

Is it not to clothe the naked, to procure for them a garment of light, a raiment of glory?

Is it not an admirable degree of hospitality, to procure their admission into the heavenly Jerusalem, and to make them fellow citizens with the saints and domestics of God?

Is it not a greater service to place souls in Heaven, than to bury bodies in the earth?

As to spirituals, is it not a work whose merit may be compared to that of counseling the weak, correcting the wayward, instructing the ignorant, forgiving offences, enduring injuries? And what consolation, however great, that can be given to the afflicted of this world, is comparable with that which is brought by our prayers, to those poor souls who have such bitter need of them?

4. Motives on account of which Imperfect Christians Ought Not to Fear Their Passage to Eternity, and May Even Desire It [4]

As the Christian life is only an imitation and expression of the life which Jesus Christ led for us, so the Christian death ought to be only an imitation and expression of the death which Jesus Christ endured for us. Jesus Christ died to satisfy the justice of God for the sins of all men, and to put an end to the reign of iniquity, to render to His Father the most perfect obedience, by submitting to the sentence of death justly pronounced against all sinners, whose place He held, to render by His death an infinite homage to the majesty of God, and to acknowledge His sovereign dominion over all creatures. Every Christian is obliged to accept death in these same dispositions, and should esteem himself only too happy in the thought that Jesus Christ wished to unite the Sacrifice of His divine life, infinitely more precious than the lives of all men and angels, with the sacrifice which each one of us should make to God of our miserable and unworthy life, and that He wished to render our death,

---

4 We have so often met, in the exercise of our holy ministry, with souls who have an excessive fear of death, that we have thought it a duty to add to the consoling reflections of St. Francis de Sales another chapter, the most solid we know on the subject. [This note and this section appear to have been written by Fr. Huguet, the compiler.—*Publisher,* 2013.]

by uniting it with His, capable of meriting for us an eternal life. To die without participating in these dispositions of Jesus Christ at death, is not to die as a Christian, it is to die of necessity as a beast, it is to die as the reprobate.[5]

Every Christian is obliged to labor for the acquisition of these dispositions during his whole life, which is only given him to learn how to die well. We should often adore in Jesus Christ that ardent zeal which He had to satisfy the justice of God and to destroy sin, that spirit of obedience and sacrifice in which He lived and died, and which He still retains in the mystery of the Eucharist. We should ask Him to share it with us, especially during the time of the Holy Sacrifice of the Mass and Communion, when Jesus Christ offers Himself again to His Father in these same dispositions, and comes to us to communicate them to us. The more we participate in these holy dispositions, the less we shall fear a death which ought to be most precious and meritorious before God, and which will be the more so, as we shall more fully enter into the designs of Jesus Christ, who, dying really but once, to render to His Father the supreme honor which was due to Him, desired to offer to Him till the end of ages the death of each of His members, as a continuation of His sacrifice.

One of the chief effects of the Incarnation and death of Jesus Christ has been to deliver us from the fear of death: He became man, and a mortal man, *that He might destroy by His death him who was the prince of death, that is to say, the devil, and that He might deliver those whom the fear of*

---

5 A Christian would implicitly participate in these dispositions simply by being in the state of grace.—*Publisher,* 2013.

death held in continual servitude during life. Is it not in some manner to dishonor the victory of Jesus Christ over death, to tremble before an enemy whom He has vanquished, and to remain still in slavery through fear of dying?

Jesus Christ ardently desired the arrival of the hour that would consummate His sacrifice, by the effusion of His blood: "I have a baptism," so He calls His Passion, "wherewith I am to be baptized, and how am I straitened until it be accomplished!" Should not a Christian, who has the honor of being one of His members, enter into His spirit, and desire the accomplishment of the baptism with which he is to be baptized? For death ought to appear to the true Christian as a baptism, in which he is to be washed from all his sins, and regenerated to a life of immortality, perfectly exempt from every corruption of sin. We should, then, like Jesus, desire with ardor to sacrifice our life as soon as possible: firstly, to render to the sovereign majesty of God, and all His divine perfections, the greatest glory that any creature can render to Him, and to render the most perfect homage to the death of Jesus Christ, our God and Saviour; secondly, to offer to God the most worthy thanksgiving, in gratitude for having sacrificed for us the life of His Son on the cross, as well as for having continued during so many ages to immolate His Body and Blood on our altars, and in gratitude for having given us His Holy Spirit and the life of grace, which is more precious than all the lives in the world; thirdly, to offer to God the fullest satisfaction that we are able to offer Him for our sins, by offering Him our death in union with that of Jesus Christ; fourthly, to draw down upon ourselves the greatest mercies of God, by an humble acceptance of death, and by the continual sacrifice which we shall make to Him of our life. For, although our life is so vile a thing, so little worthy of being offered to God in sacrifice, defiled as it is with so many sins, yet it is the most considerable present we can make to Him; and God is so good as to receive this remnant of sin, as a sacrifice of sweet odor.

A countless number of martyrs, of every age, sex, and country, have run to death with joy, and looked upon it as their greatest happiness to be able to sacrifice themselves for God in the midst of the most dreadful torments. The pagan or irregular life which some among them had led previously did not stay their ardor; because they hoped by their death entirely to repair the past. "Why," says St. Jerome, "do we not imitate them in something?" Are we not, like them, the disciples of a God crucified for our salvation, and destined to the same kingdom of Heaven? It is true that we have not, like them, the happiness of offering to God a bloody death; but, why should we not endeavor to supply its place, by the continual oblation that we can make to Him of the kind of death which He destines for us? "For I venture to say," adds this holy father, "that there is as much, and perhaps more, merit in offering to Him our life during the successive moments in which He preserves it to us, than in losing it once by the cruelty of executioners. The sacrifice which we make to God of our life, if sincere, is the greatest act of love that we can make." St. Augustine says: "If the angels could envy any privilege in man, it is his ability to die for the love of God."

We ask of God every day that His kingdom should

come. This kingdom of God will be perfectly established in us only by death, which will be for each of us an end to sin, the destruction of concupiscence, and the beginning of the absolute reign of justice and charity. To ask of God, every day, the coming of His kingdom, and, at the same time, to fear death excessively—are these things easily allied? The desire of the kingdom of God and of eternal life is essential to salvation. "It is not sufficient," says St. Augustine, "to believe by faith in a blessed life, we must love it by charity, and wish that we were already in the celestial abode; and it is impossible to have these dispositions in the heart, without being glad to depart from this life." At the commencement of the divine prayer in which we ask of God the coming of His kingdom, He orders us to say to Him: "Our Father, Who art in Heaven." If we sincerely believe that God is our Father, and we His children, how can we fear to go to our Heavenly Father, in order to reign with Him, to enjoy His possessions, and to repose forever on His bosom?

The Scripture represents all the faithful as so many persons who expect the last coming of Jesus Christ, who love His coming, and who go forward to meet Him as far as lies in them by their groans and desires. Why are we Christians? Why are we converted to God? "It is," says St. Paul, "to serve the true and living God, and to expect the Heaven of His Son Jesus, whom He has raised up, and who has delivered us from the wrath to come." To whom will the Lord, *as a just judge, render the crown of justice on the great day?* The same Apostle answers, that it will be *to those who love His coming. Since the earth, and all that it contains, must be consumed by fire,* which will precede the coming of the great Judge, "What ought you to be," says St. Peter to all the faithful, "and what ought to be the sanctity of your life, the piety of your actions, awaiting, and, as it were, hastening by your desires, the coming of the day of the Lord?" Jesus Christ, after having given a description of the frightful signs which will precede His coming, after having told us that men will wither away for fear in expectation of the evils with which the world of the impious will be threatened, addresses immediately to all His disciples who were present, and to all those who should follow Him during the course of ages, these sweet words of consolation and joy: "As for you, when these things begin to happen, look up, and lift up your heads, because your redemption is at hand. . . . When you shall see these things come to pass, know that the kingdom of God is nigh." The great maxims which the Apostles and Jesus Christ Himself teach us, accord perfectly with an ardent desire of death; but do they accord with an excessive fear of death? Are we not afraid to dishonor those great truths, by the opposition that we show between the dispositions which they require, and those which we entertain? "Jesus Christ," says St. Augustine, "will share His kingdom with all those who shall have sincerely desired that His kingdom should come." "He will render," says the Apostle, "the crown of justice to those who love His coming." What, then, should we desire more than His arrival, since it is the sure means of our reigning with Him?

Many persons are tormented at death with the remembrance of their crimes, and, seeing that they have done no penance, they are tempted to despair. "Oh, if I had fasted! Oh, if I had performed great charities for the poor! Alas! I am no longer in a state to perform them. What will become of me? What shall I do?" You can do something greater than all you have mentioned, namely, accept death, and unite it with that of Jesus Christ. There is no mortification comparable to this: it is the deepest humiliation, the greatest impoverishment, the most terrible penance; and I do not at all doubt but that he who is grieved for having offended God, and who accepts death willingly in satisfaction for his sins, will immediately obtain pardon. What a consolation to be able to perform while dying a greater penance than all the anchorets have been able to perform in deserts, and this at a time when one would seem no longer able to do anything! What a pity to see an innumerable multitude of persons deprive themselves of the fruit of death, which of all the pains of life is the one of most merit! *Ut quid perditio haec?*[6] Why waste so advantageous an occasion of honoring God, satisfying His justice, discharging one's debts, and purchasing Heaven?

I acknowledge that your life is nothing in comparison with that of Our Lord Jesus Christ; but, when offered through love, it is of inestimable value. What does God care about an alms of two farthings? Yet the poor widow, in the Gospel, who gave it, deserved to be praised by the Son of God, and to be preferred to the Scribes and Pharisees, who had given much more considerable alms, because, says He, she has given all that she had, and, notwithstanding her poverty, has given it with a great heart. *Haec de penuria*

---

6 "To what purpose is this waste?" (*Matt.* 26:8).—*Publisher, 2013.*

sua omnia quae habuit misit totum victum suum.[7]

We can say the same of him who gives his life to God: he gives all that he has, without reserving anything, and this is what renders death precious. This is what made the early Christians run with so much eagerness to martyrdom: they all wished to give back to Our Lord the life which they had received from Him, and to compensate by their death for that which He had endured for love of them.

We can no longer be martyrs; oh, what an affliction! but still we can die for Jesus Christ! We have a life that we can lose for His love! Oh, what a consolation!

The line of distinction which St. Augustine draws between the perfect and the imperfect is that the perfect suffer life with pain and receive death with joy, while the imperfect receive death only with patience, struggling against themselves to submit to the will of God: preferring however to yield to what He requires of them, arming themselves with courage to overcome the desire of life, and to receive death with submission and peace.

Perfection, therefore, consists in desiring to die, that we may no longer be imperfect, that we may wholly cease to offend God, that God may reign perfectly in us, and that this body of sin, which we carry about with us until death, may, in punishment of its continual revolts against God, be reduced to dust, fully to satisfy His justice and sanctity, and, by this last and most profound humiliation, fully to repair all the injuries which it has committed against the Divine Majesty. We rise towards perfection in proportion as these

---

7 "She of her want cast in all she had, even her whole living." (Cf. *Mark* 12:44). —*Publisher,* 2013.

holy desires of death become more ardent and sincere, and the quickest means of becoming perfect is to desire death with one's whole heart.

The preparations that we might wish to bring with us to our last sacrifice ought not, when the hour of consummating it arrives, to lead us to desire that the sacrifice should be deferred. These preparations are less necessary than submission to the will of God. Our submission can supply the place of these preparations, but nothing can supply the want of our submission; a thing which souls, even the most imperfect, should never forget. It is more advantageous for us to appear before Jesus Christ, when He announces His coming, than to expose ourselves to the risk of meeting Him too late, by expecting that we shall afterwards be better prepared. The essential preparation is to go before Him with confidence and love; and we must think only of exciting acts of these virtues. It ought to be a great subject of humiliation and confusion to us, not to feel a holy ardor and impatience to go to Him. Happy are we, says St. Chrysostom, if we sigh and groan continually within ourselves, awaiting the accomplishment of our divine adoption, which will be the redemption and deliverance of our bodies and souls—if we desire to depart from this world with as much ardor and impatience as the banished desire an end of their exile, and captives of their imprisonment.[8] This impatience, adds the holy doctor, which we testify to God, will serve much to obtain the pardon of our sins, and will be the best of all dispositions for appearing before Him.

---

8 Chrys., *Hom. xvii in Gen. et alib.*

We have elsewhere shown that no person, however holy his life may have been, should rely upon his virtues, if God should examine them without mercy. It is to be already condemned, to consent to be judged without a great mercy. Confidence in the divine mercy, and in the merits of Jesus Christ, is the only security for all. Since, then, we must always return to this point, let us, from this moment, abandon ourselves to these dispositions in life and in death. Let us hold, as a certain truth, that the more fully we thus abandon ourselves, the more just shall we be, and the more agreeable our sacrifices to God.